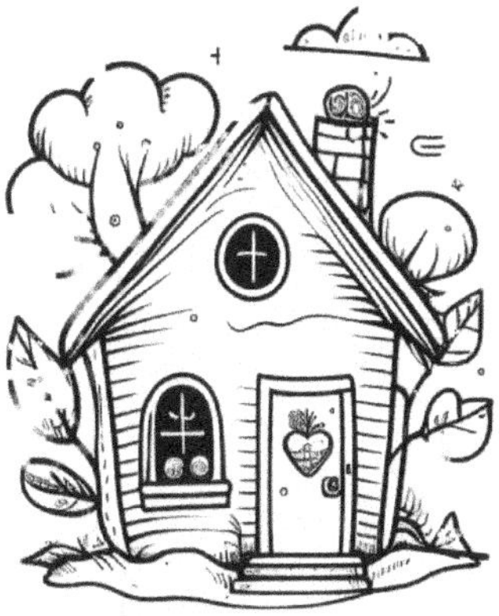

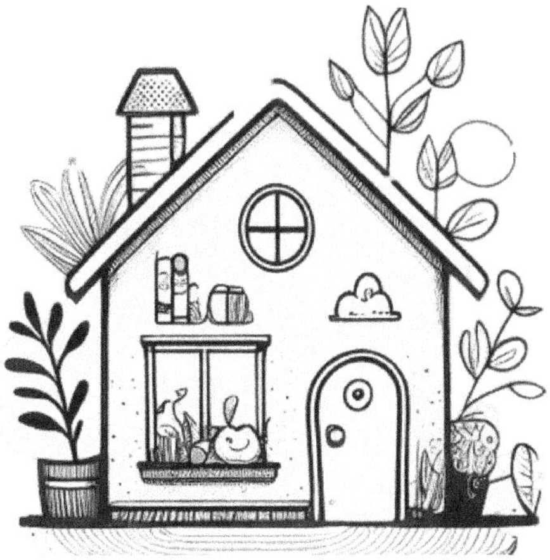

This Coloring Book Belongs to!

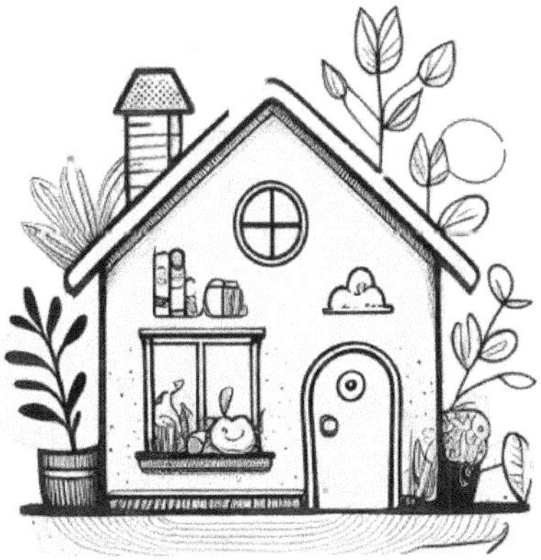

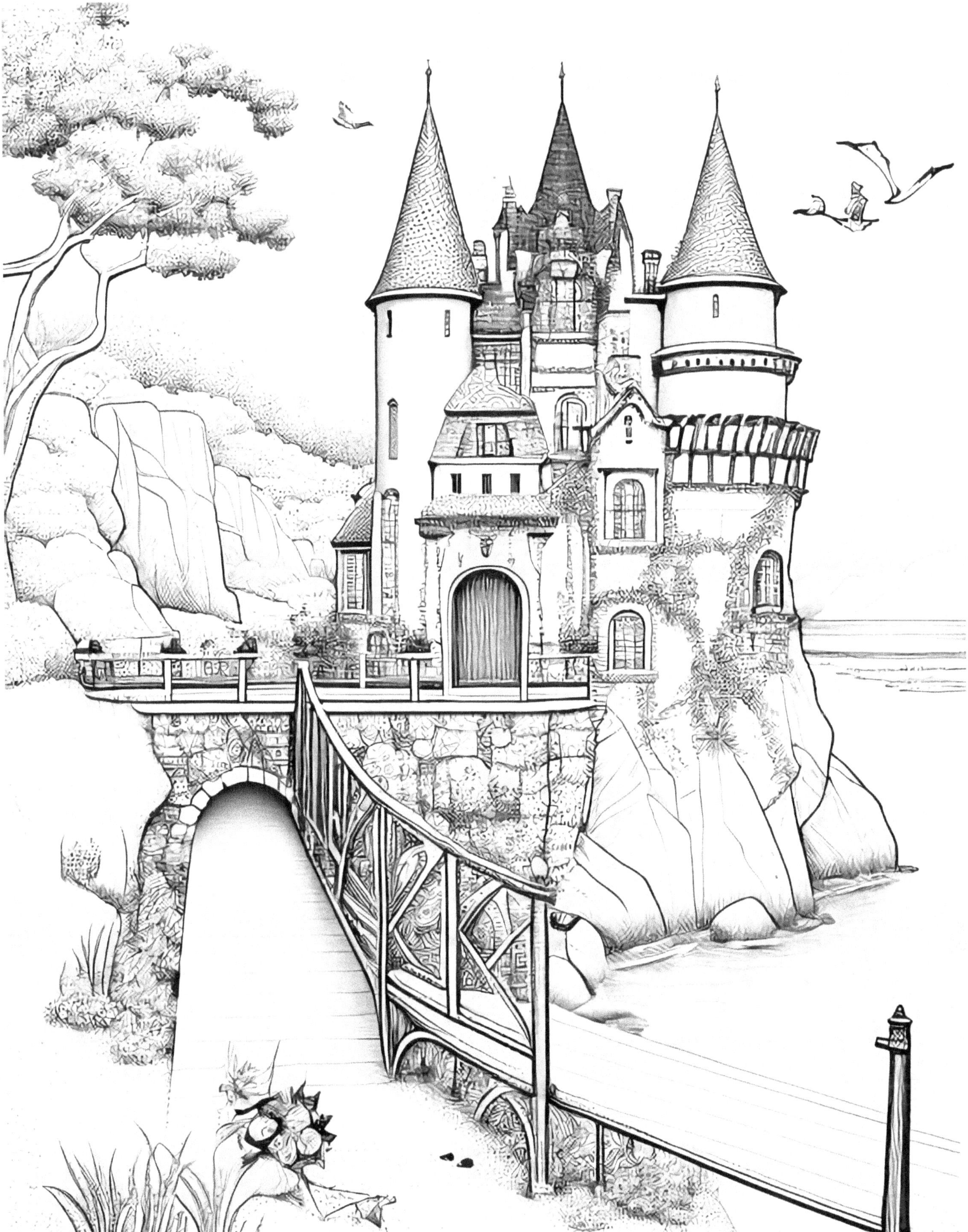

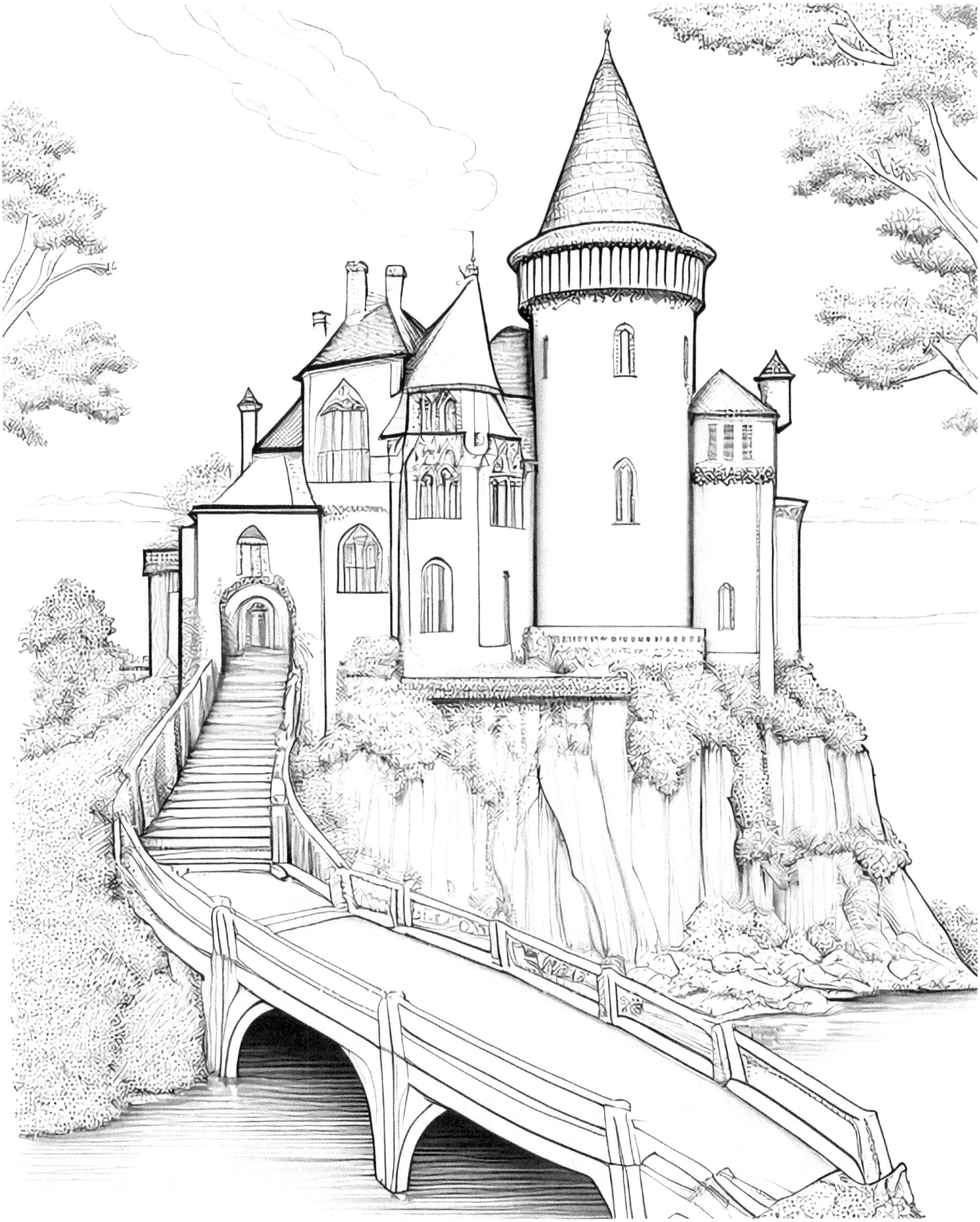

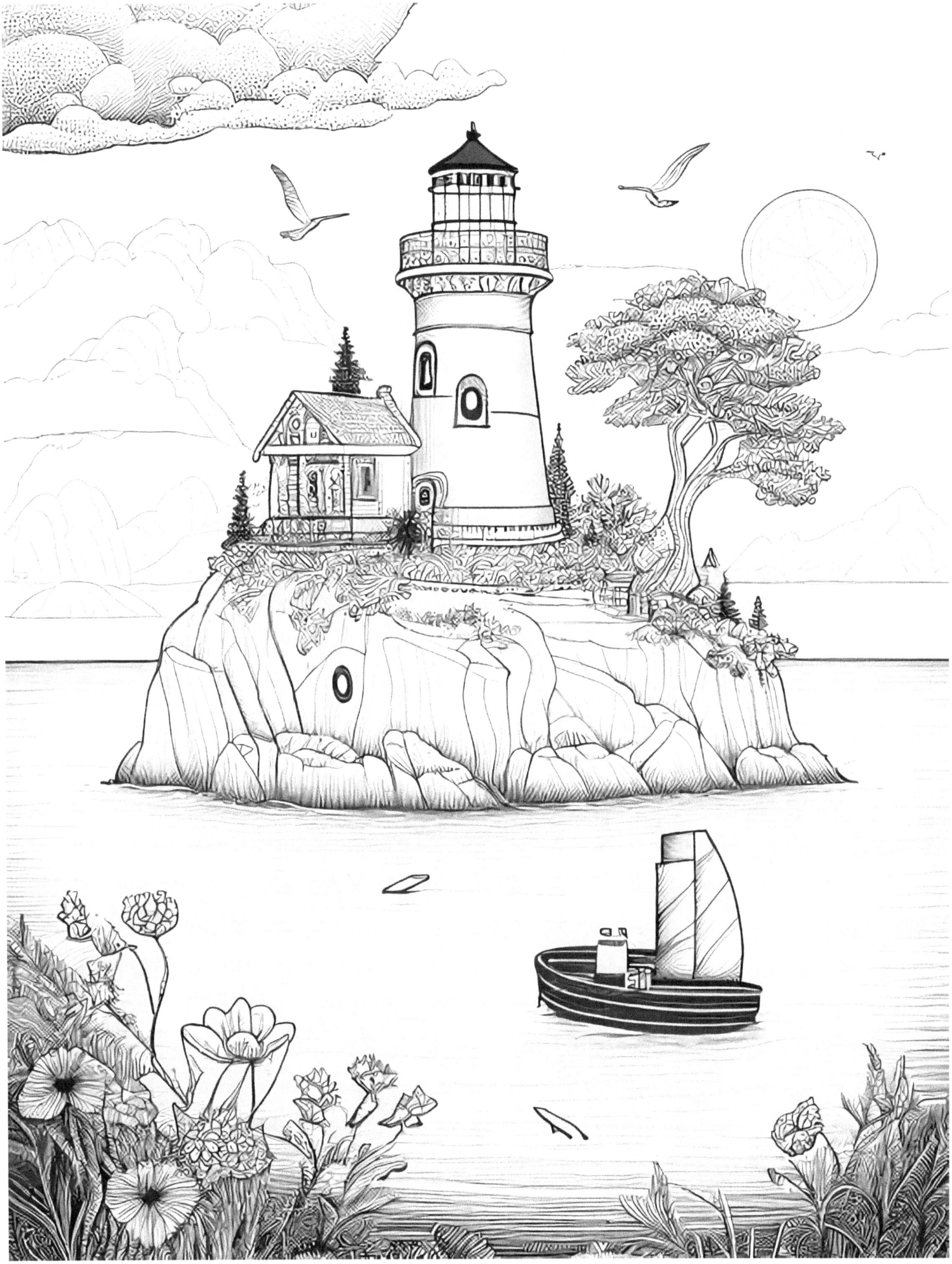

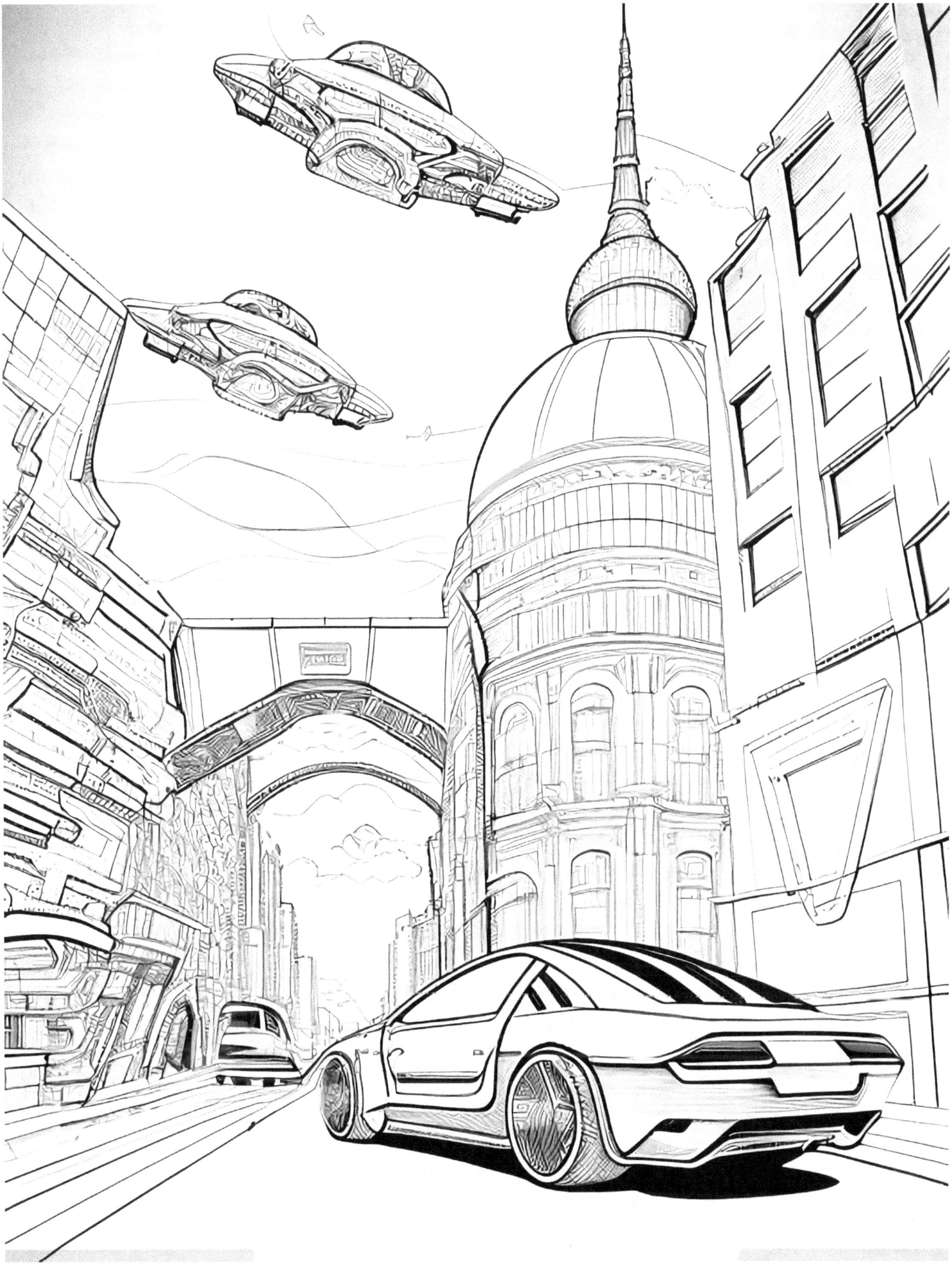

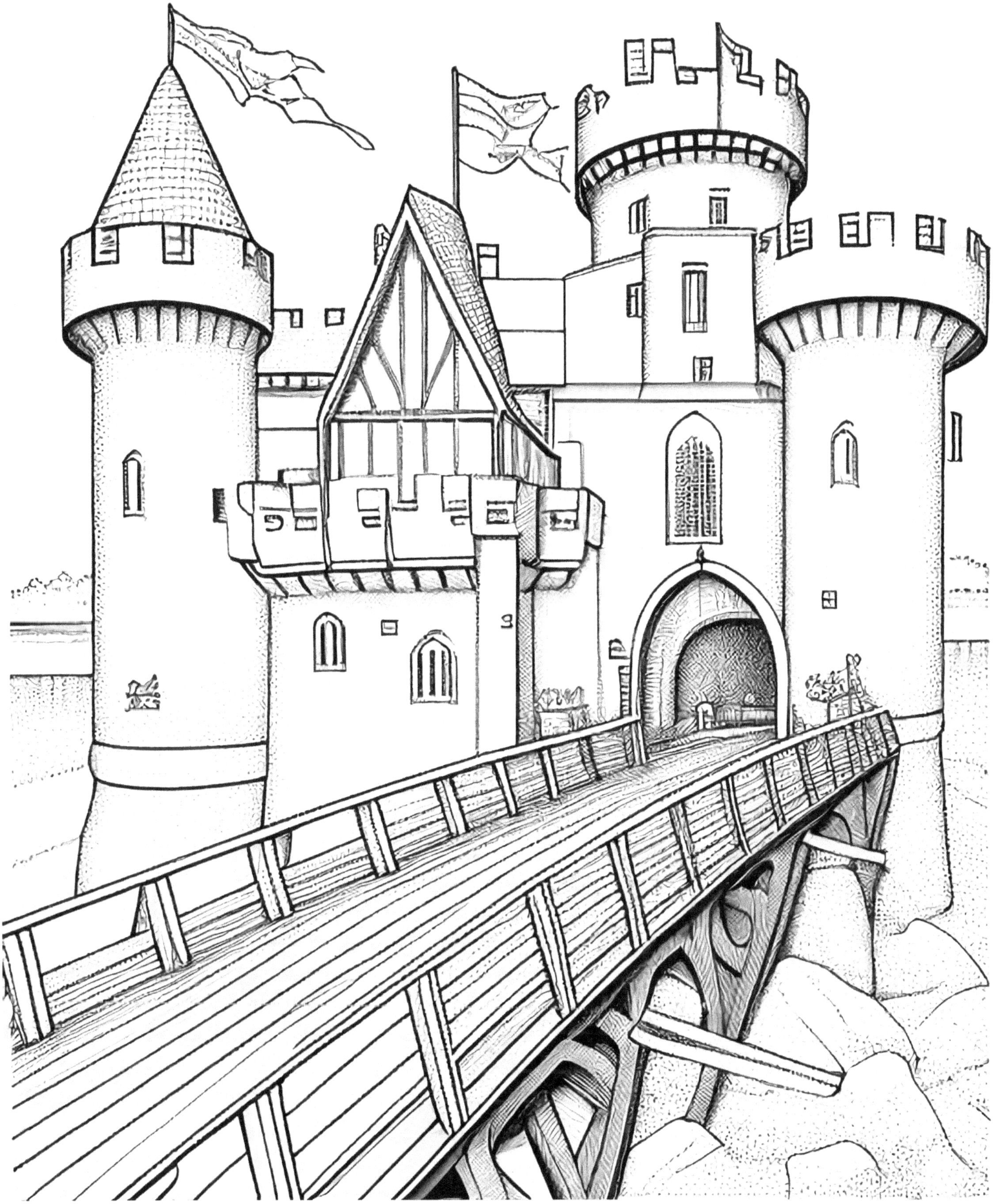

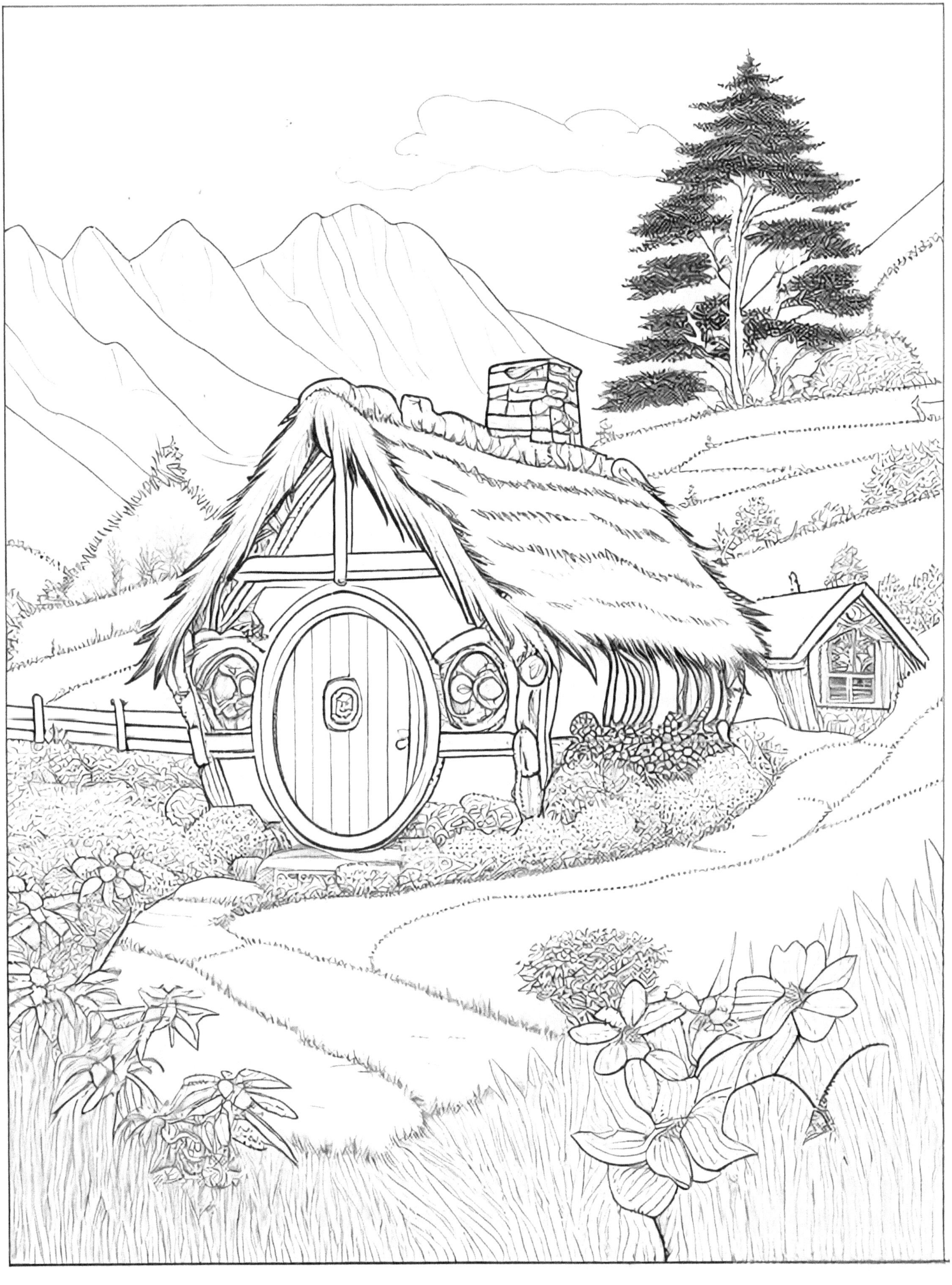

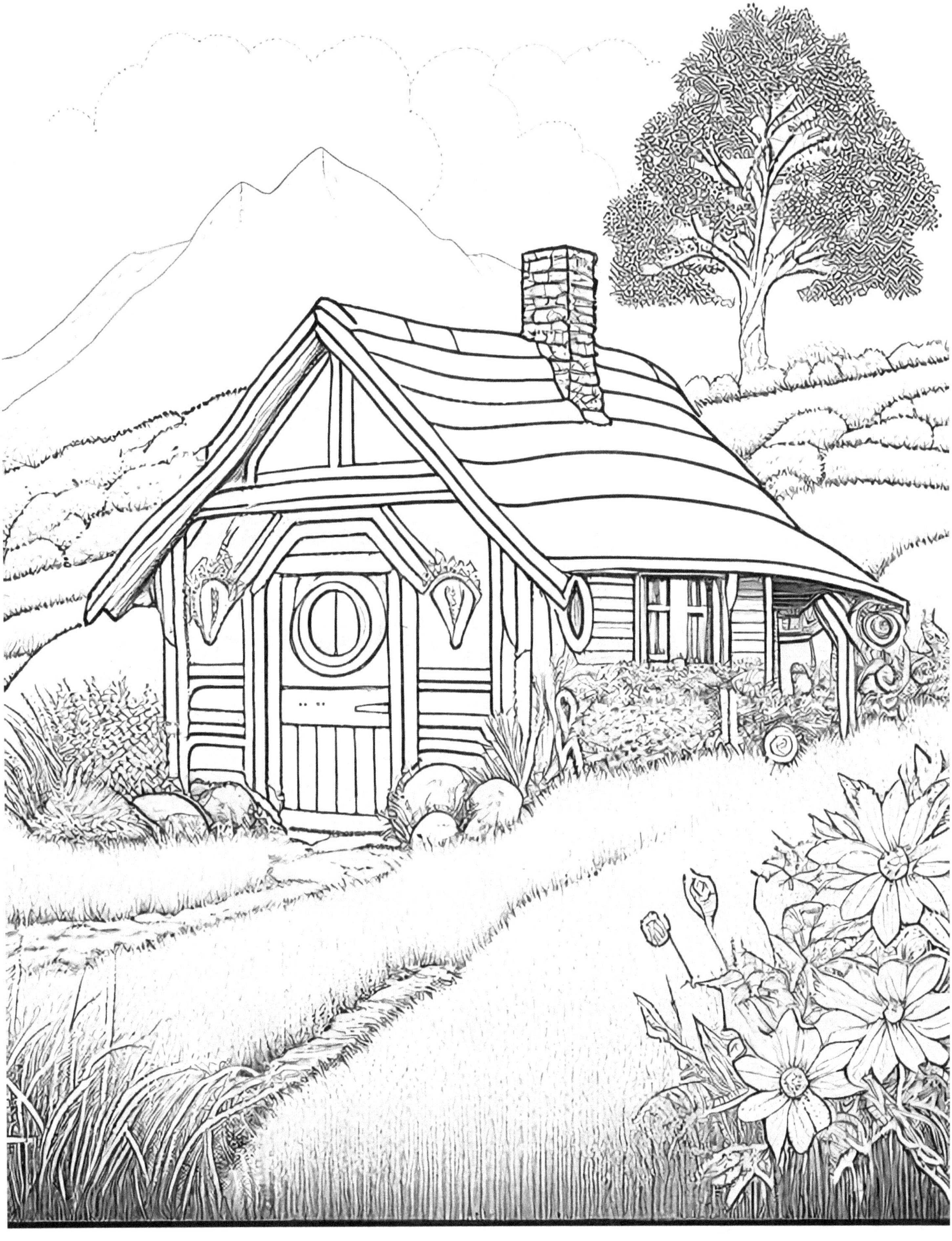

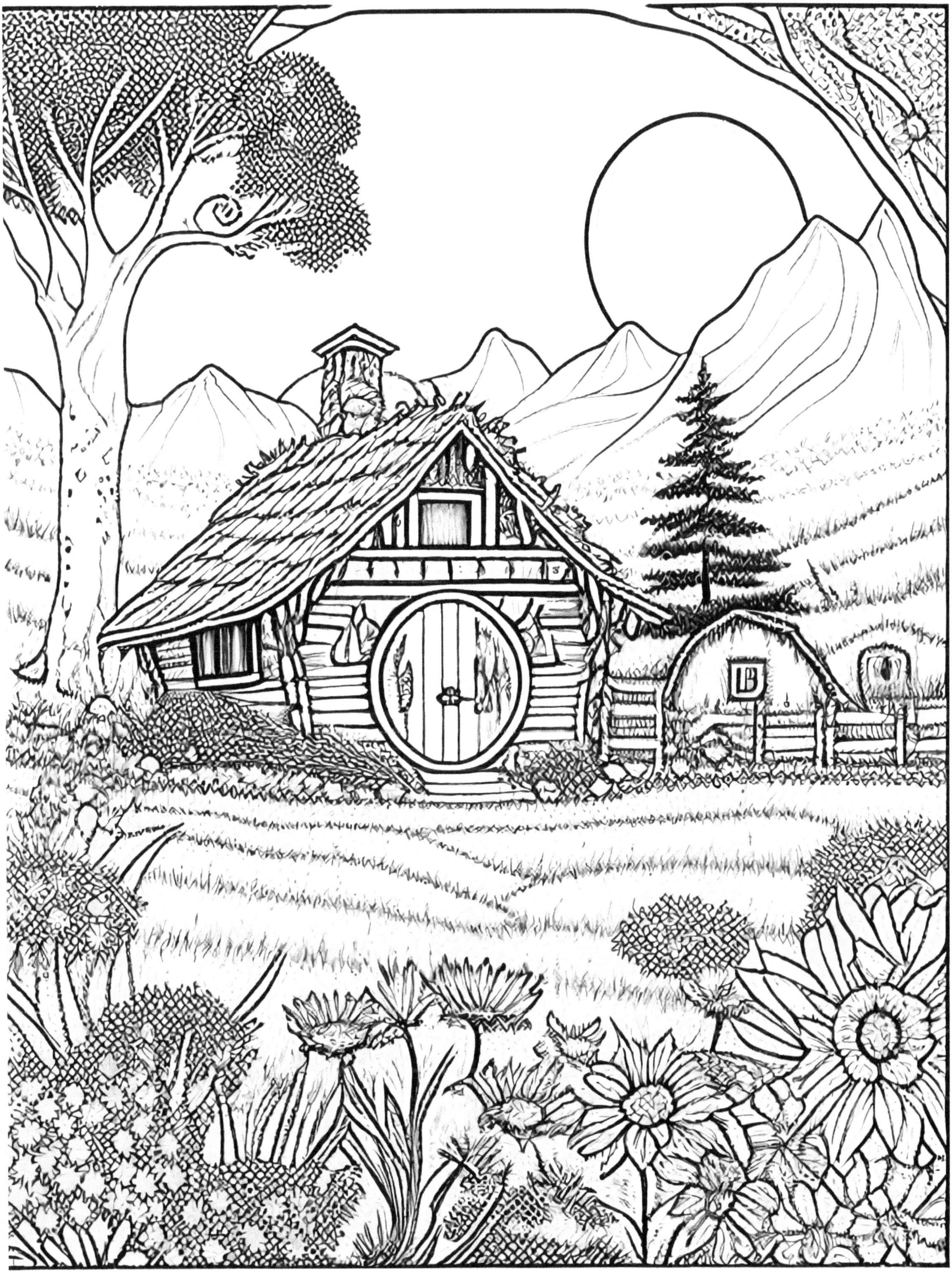

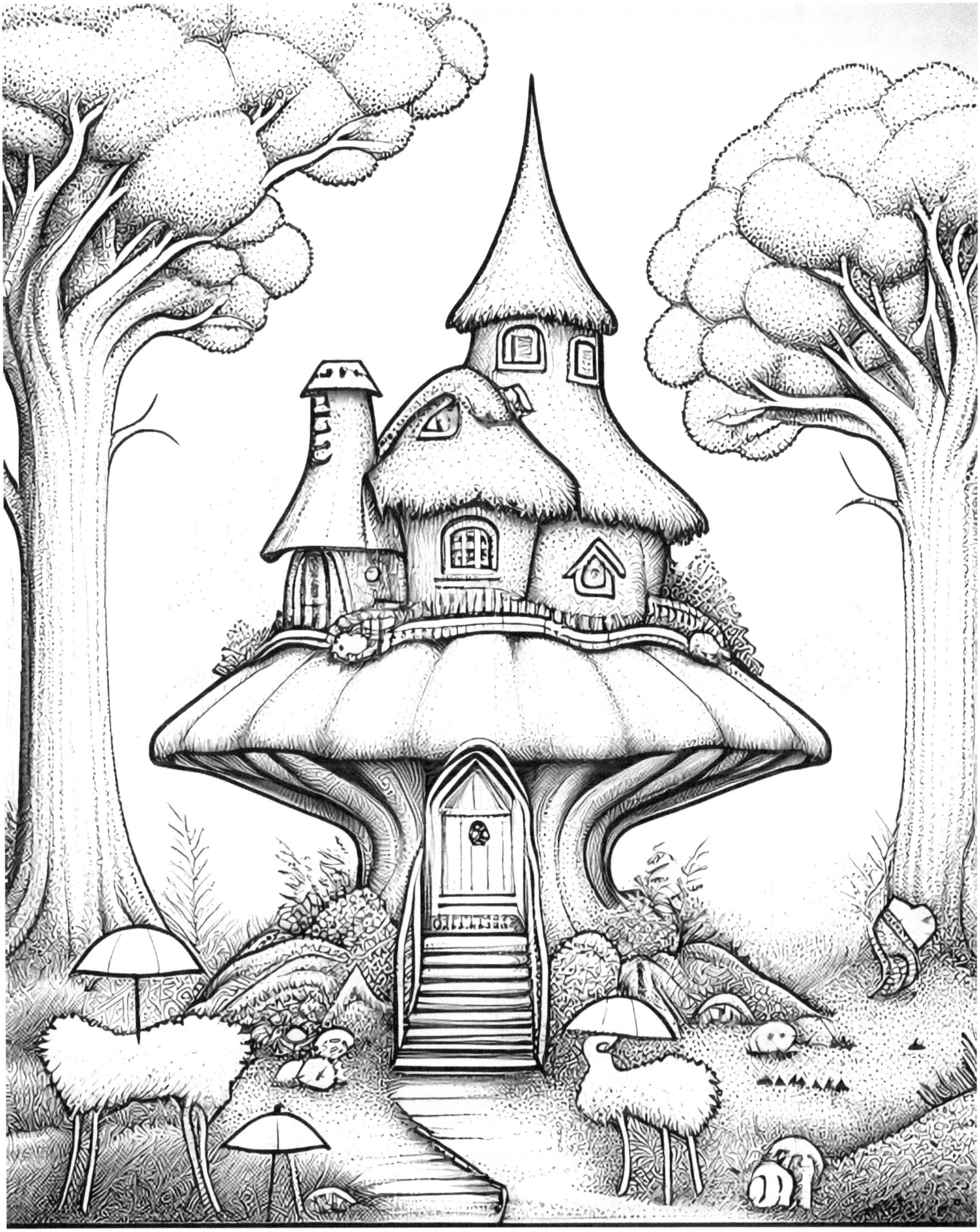

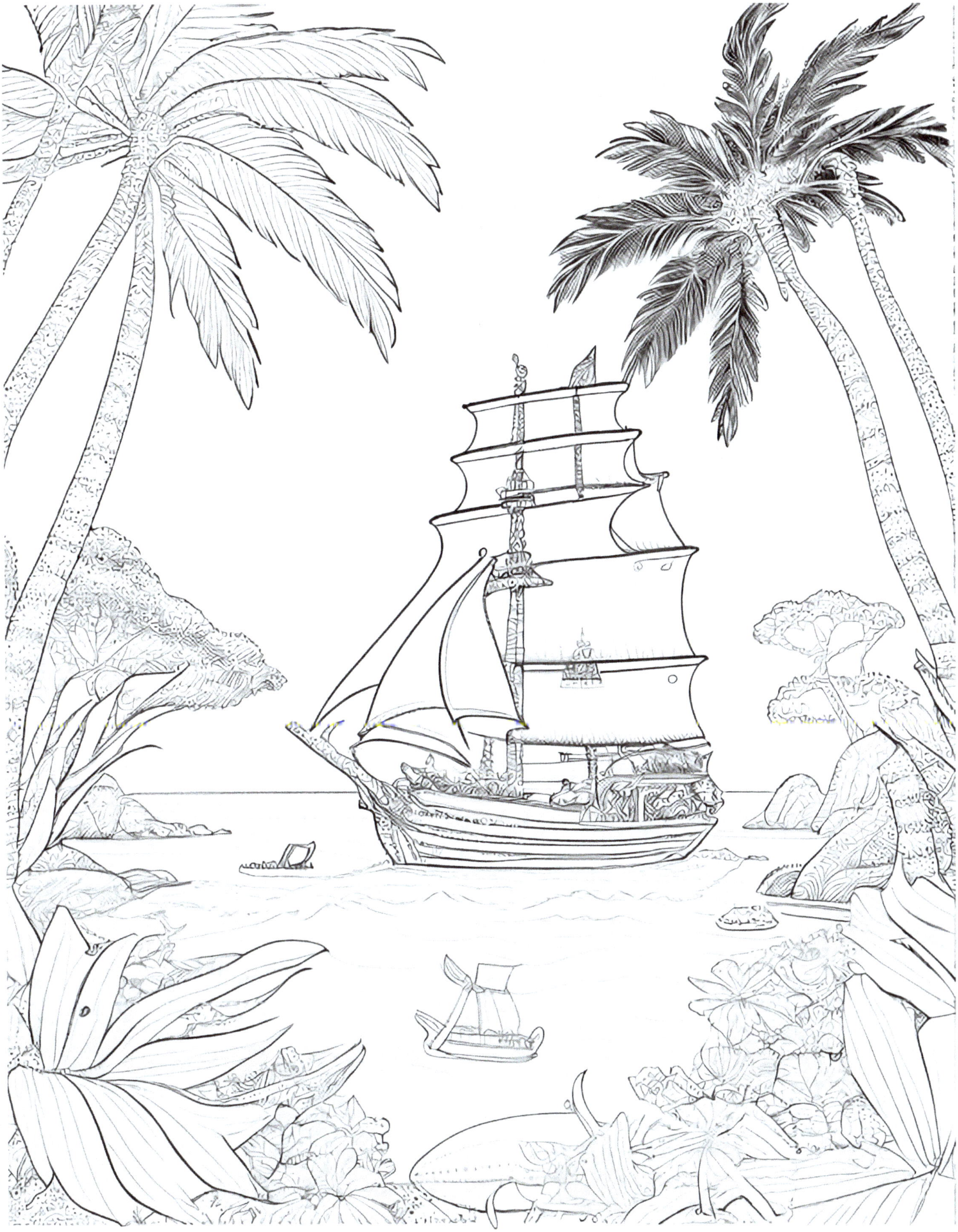

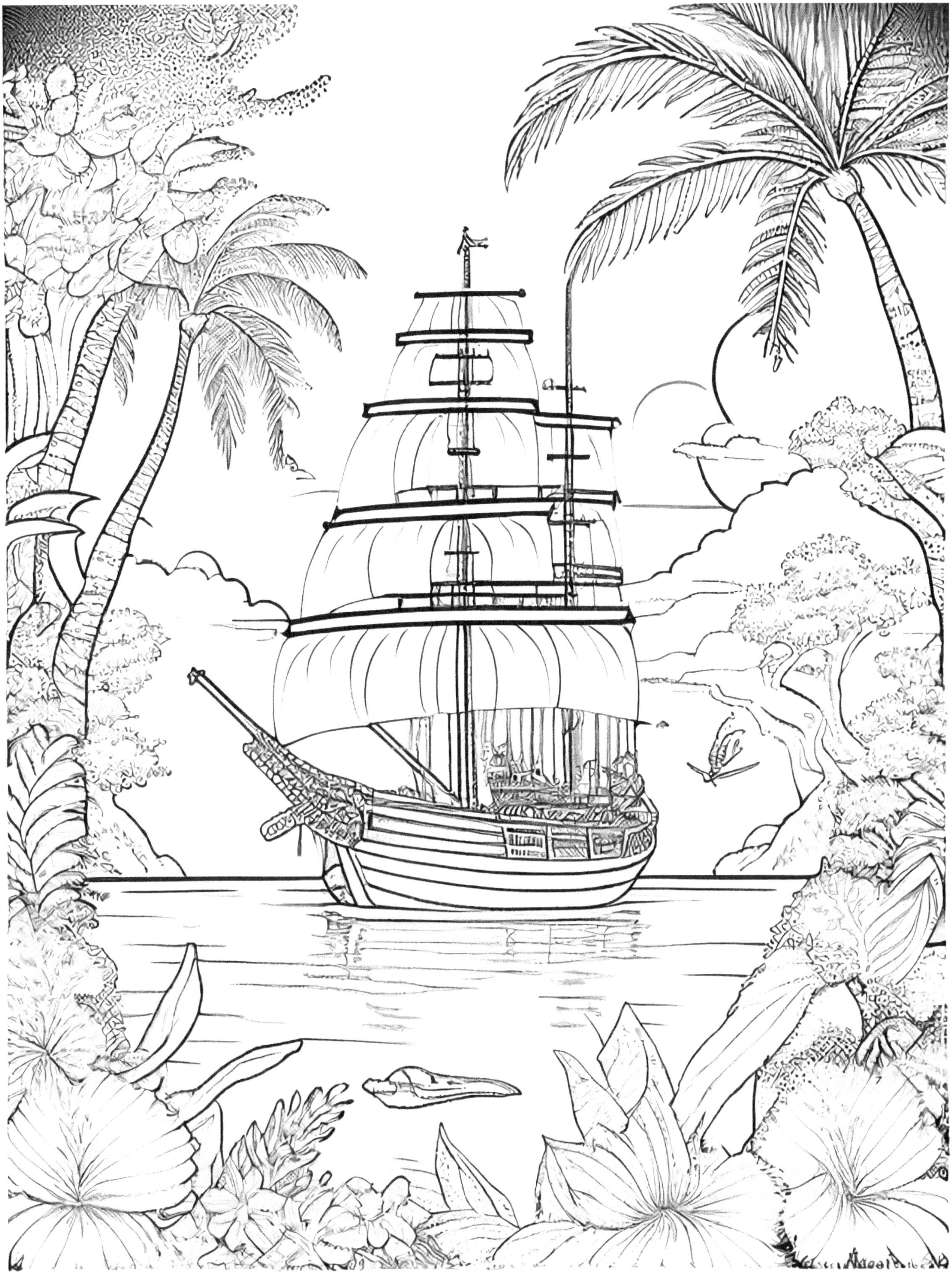

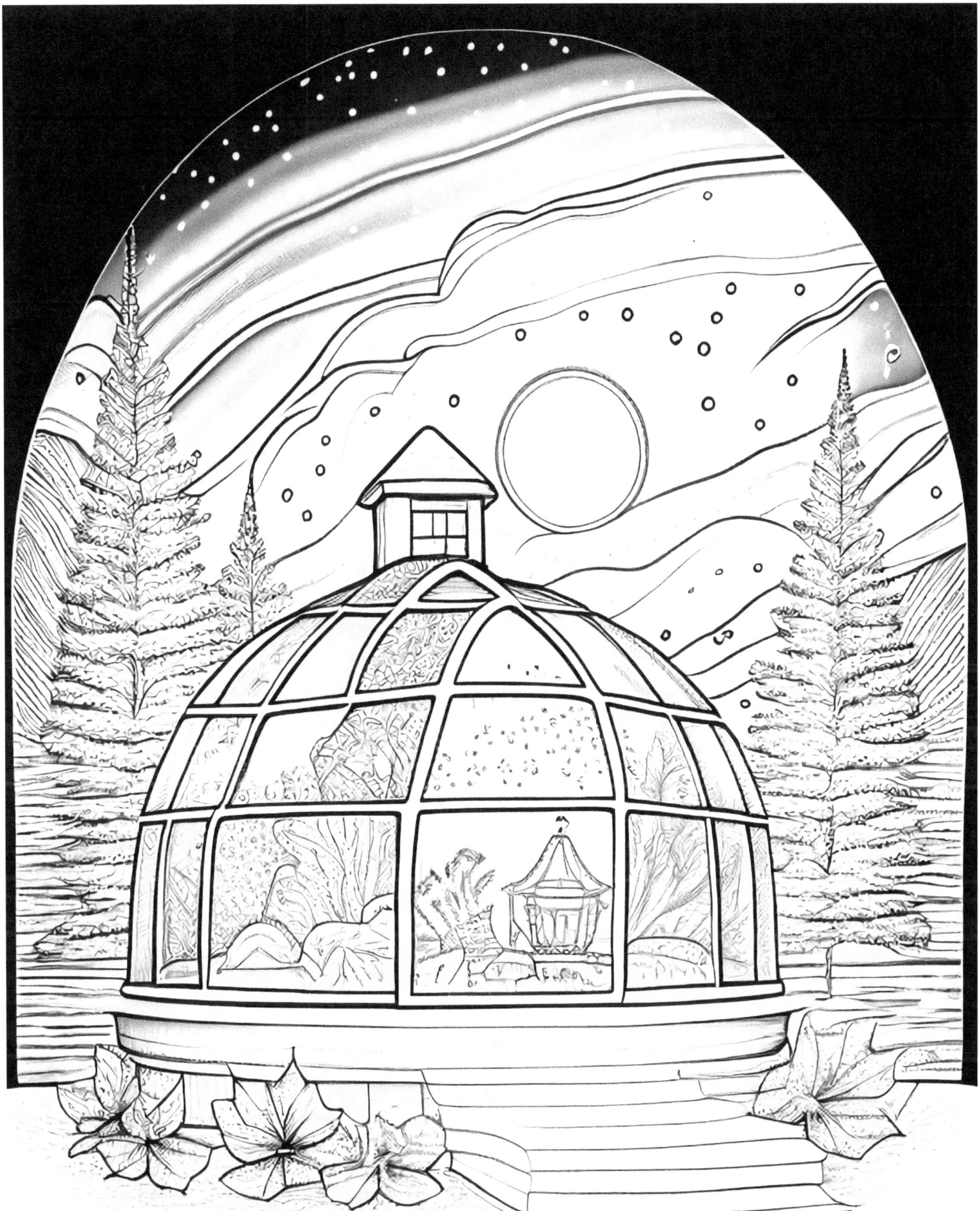

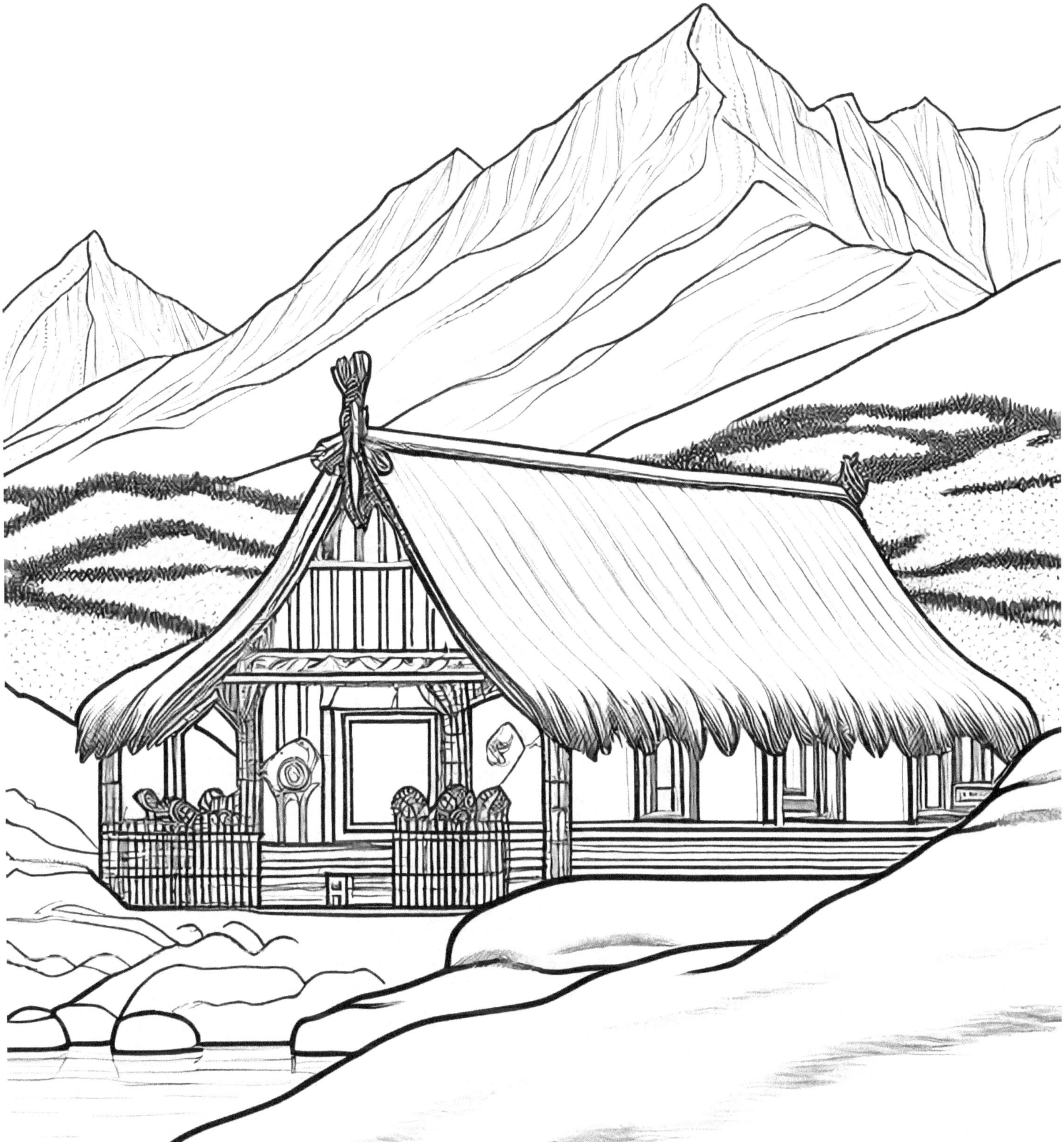

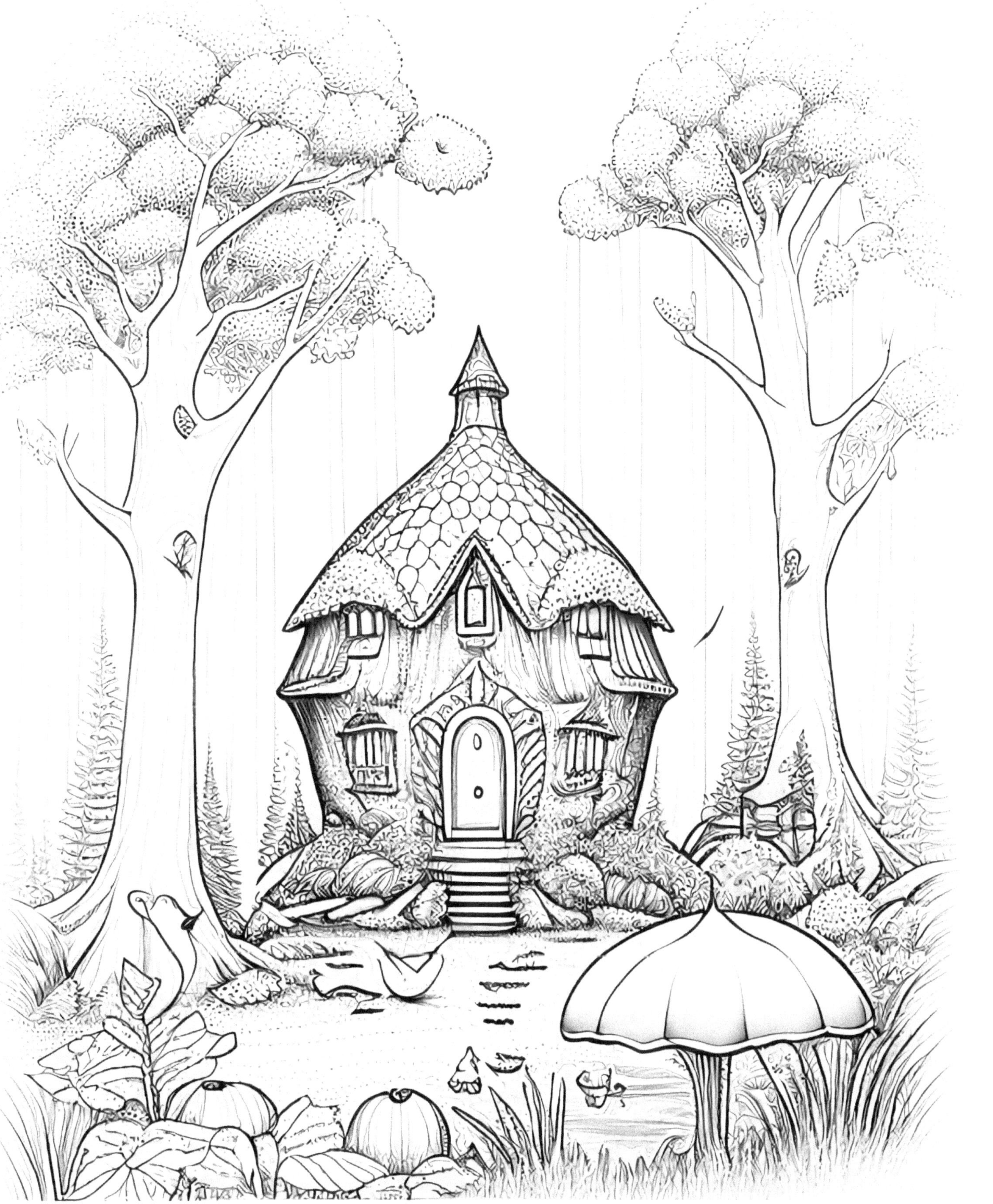

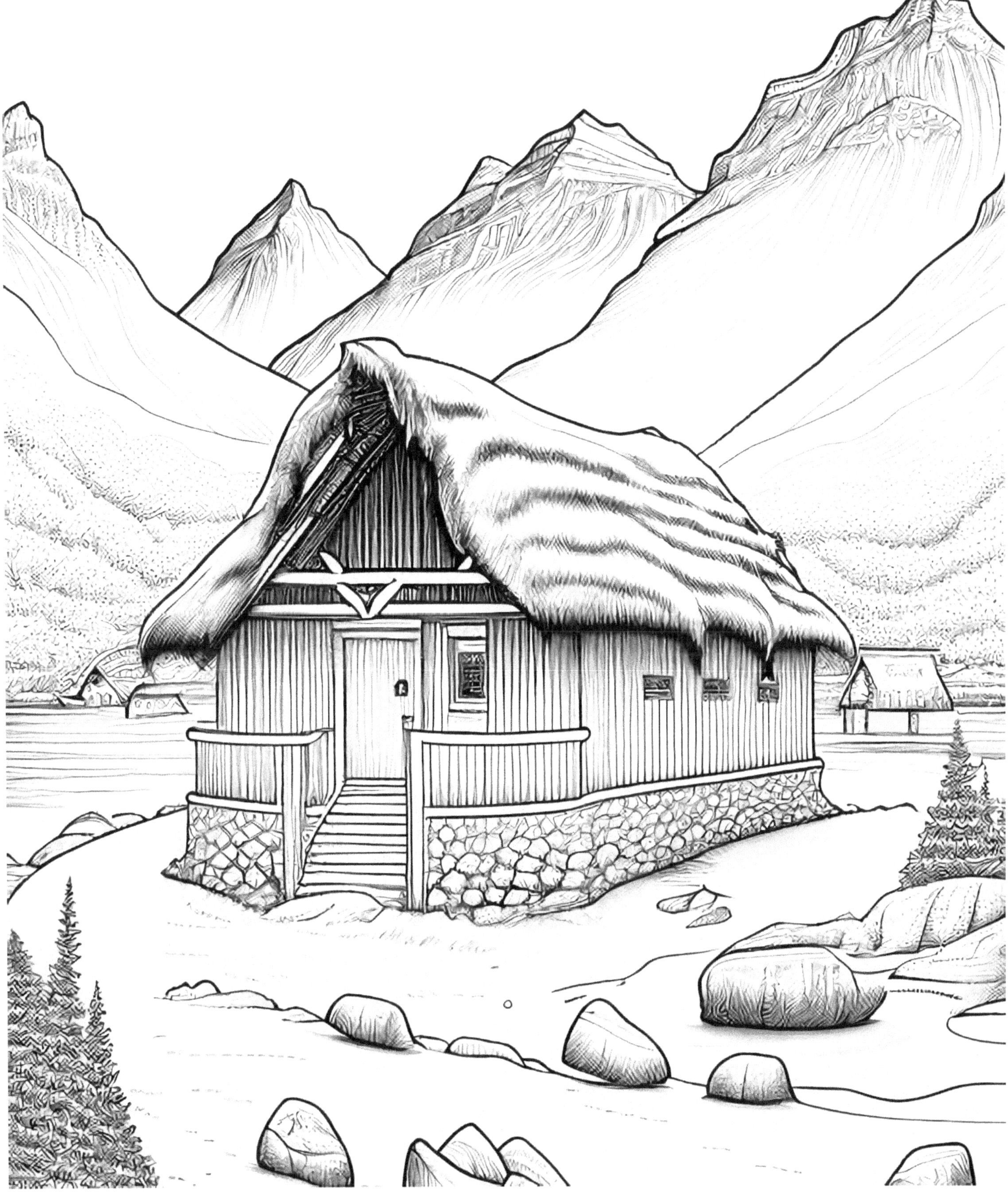

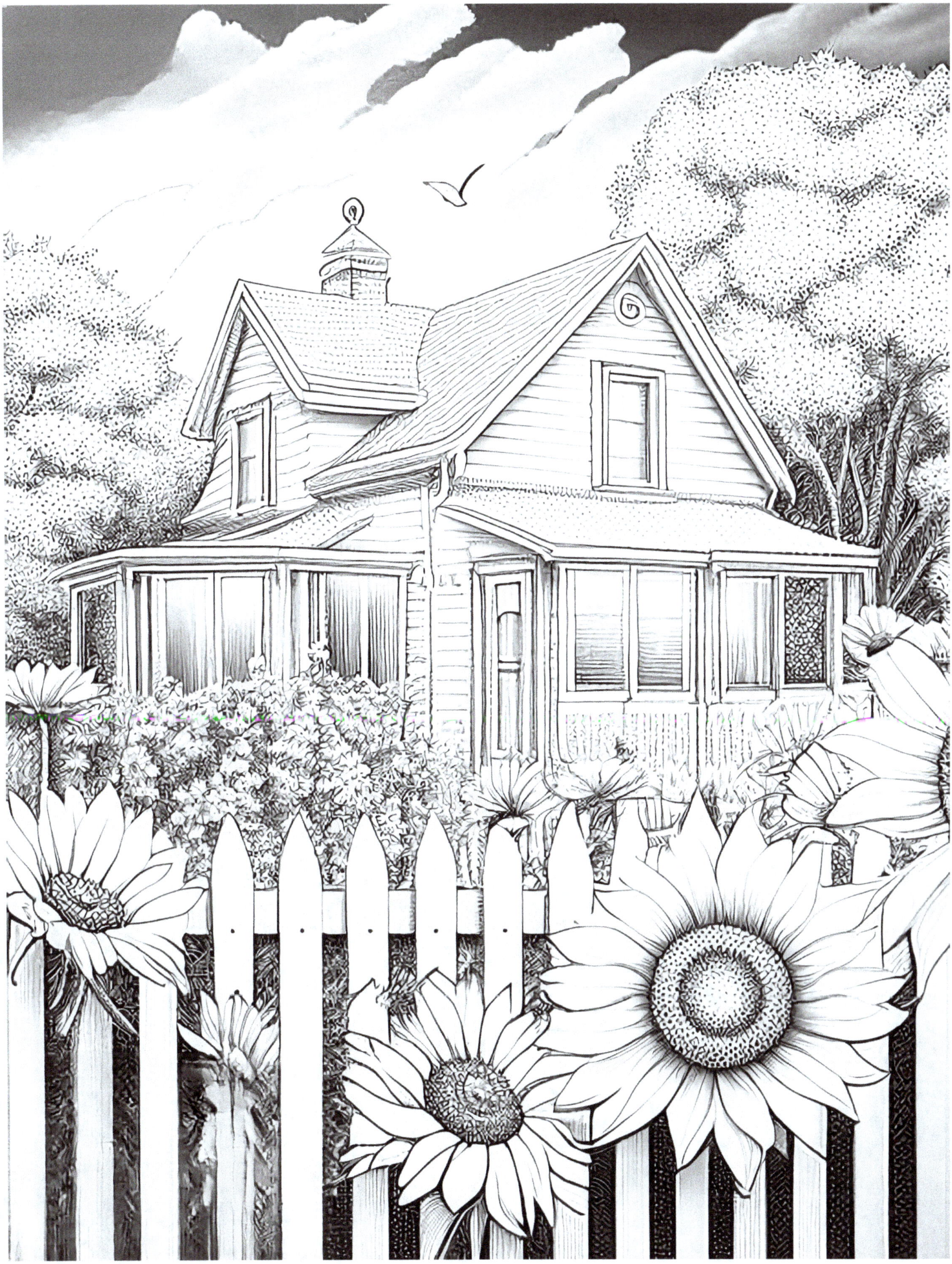

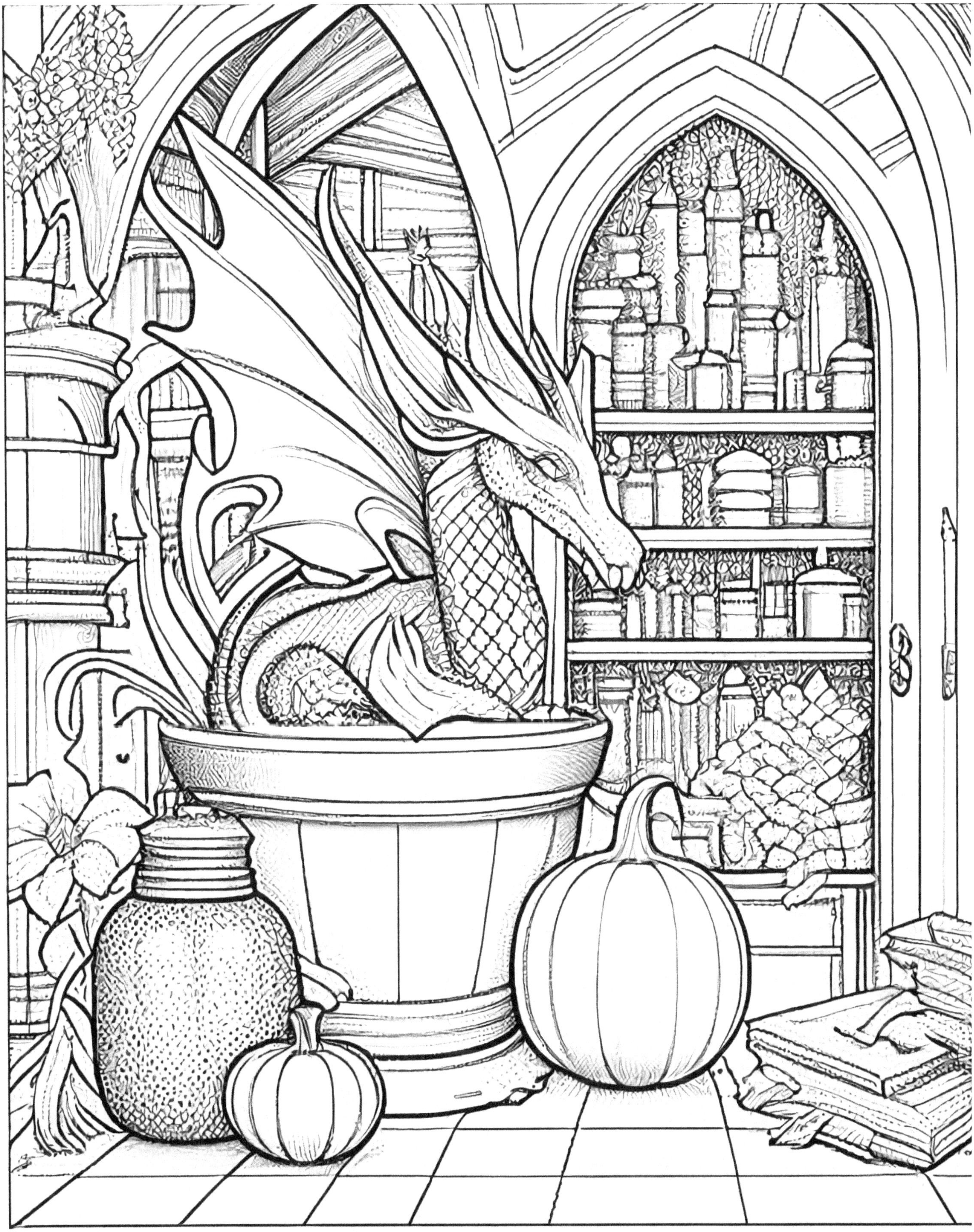

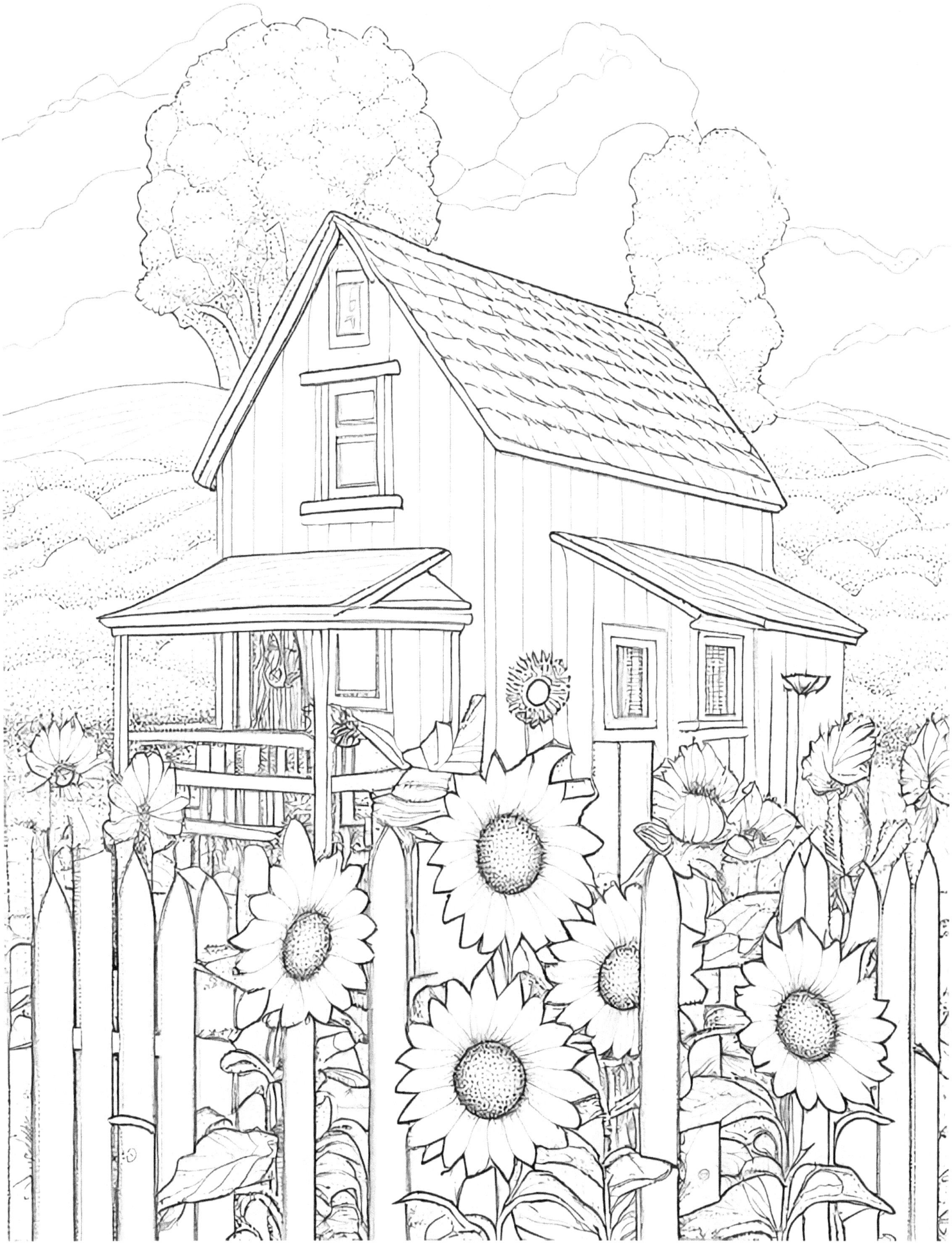

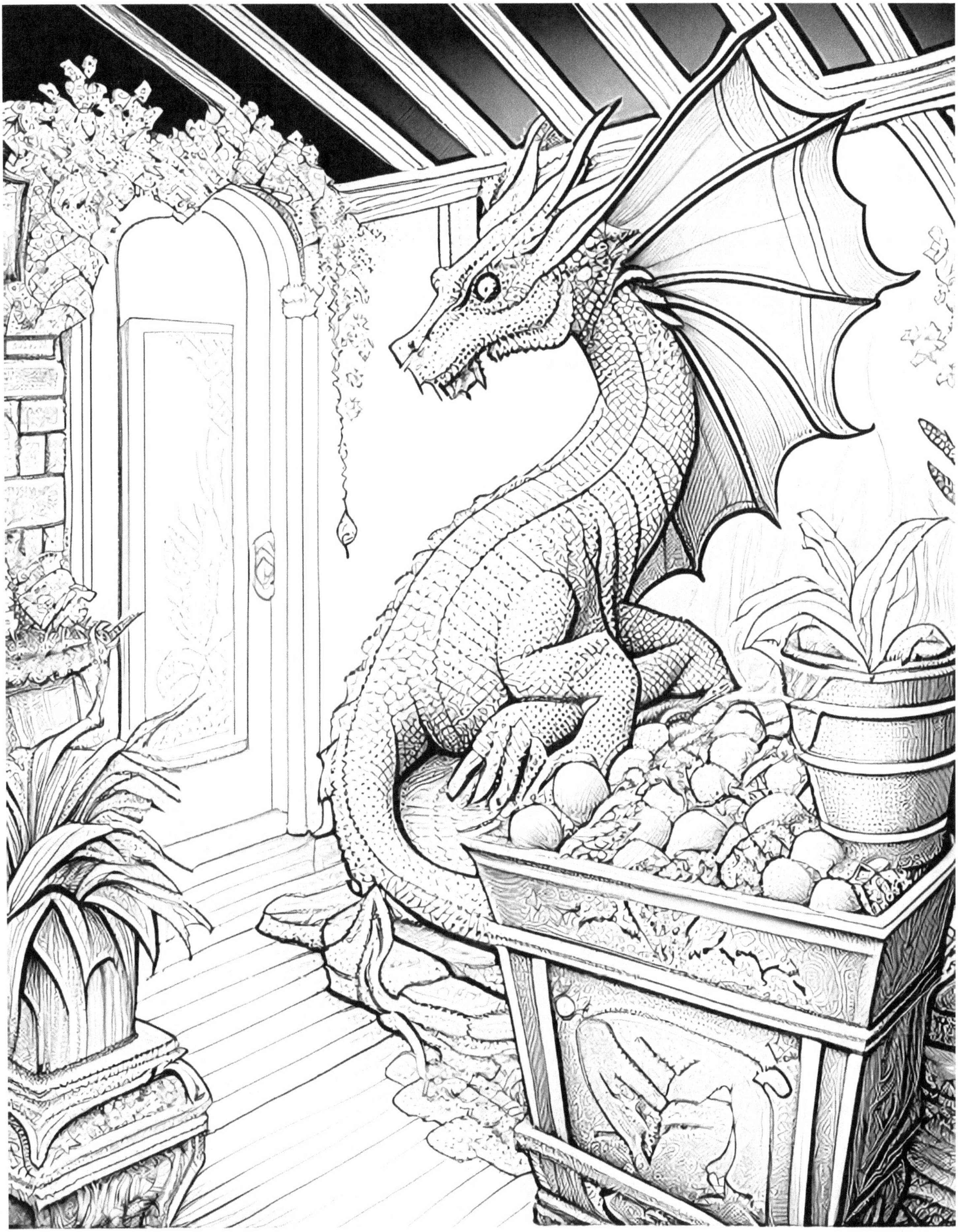

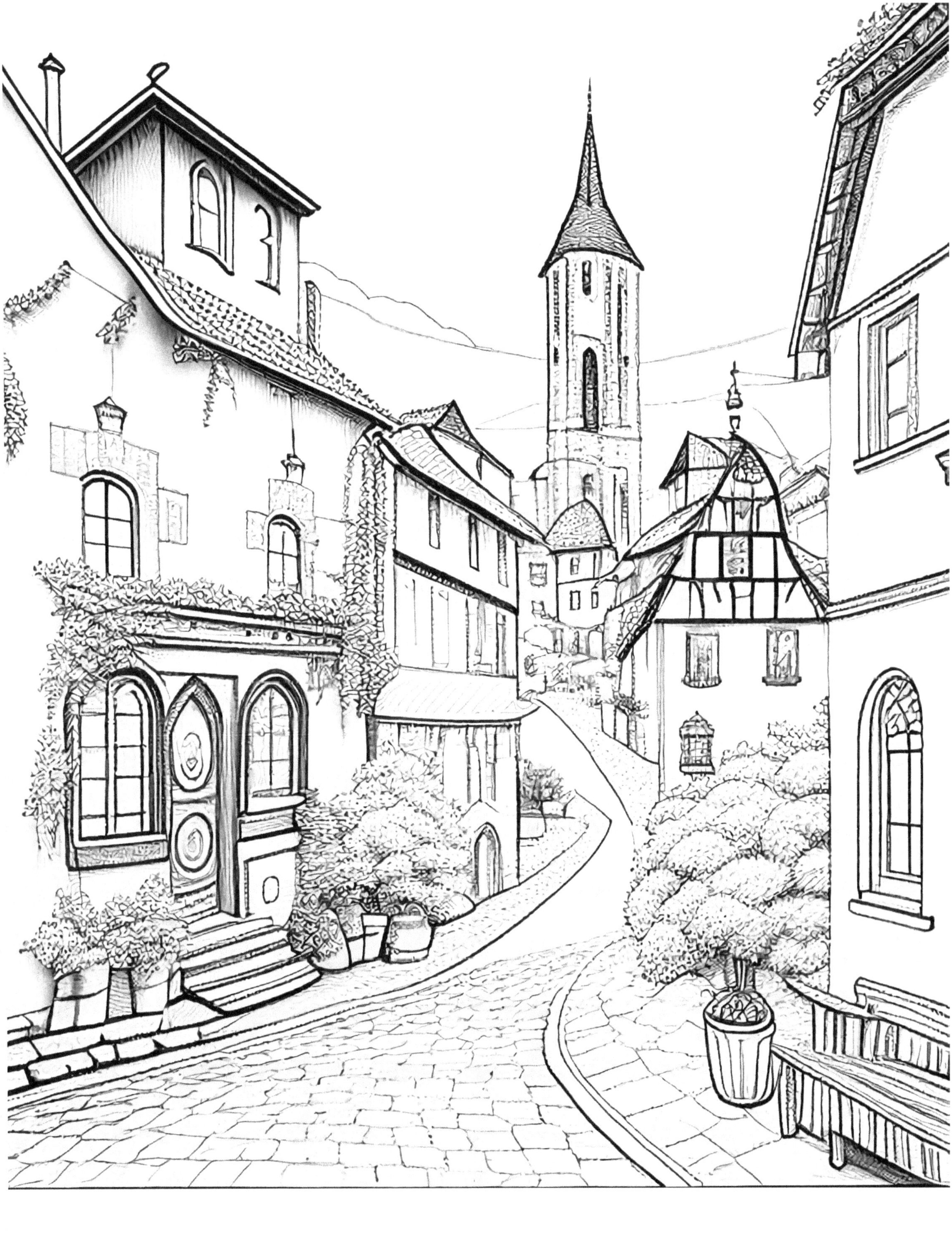

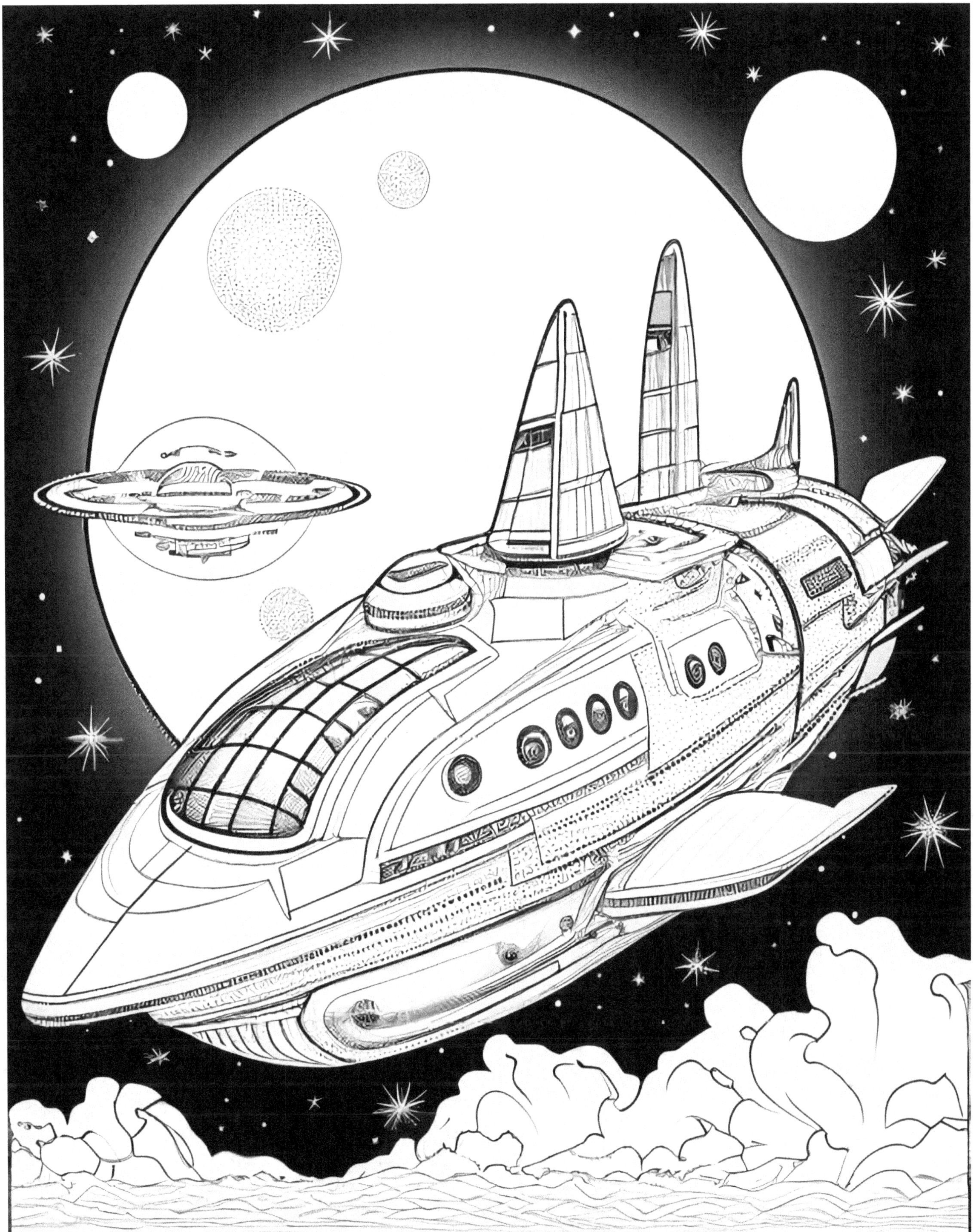

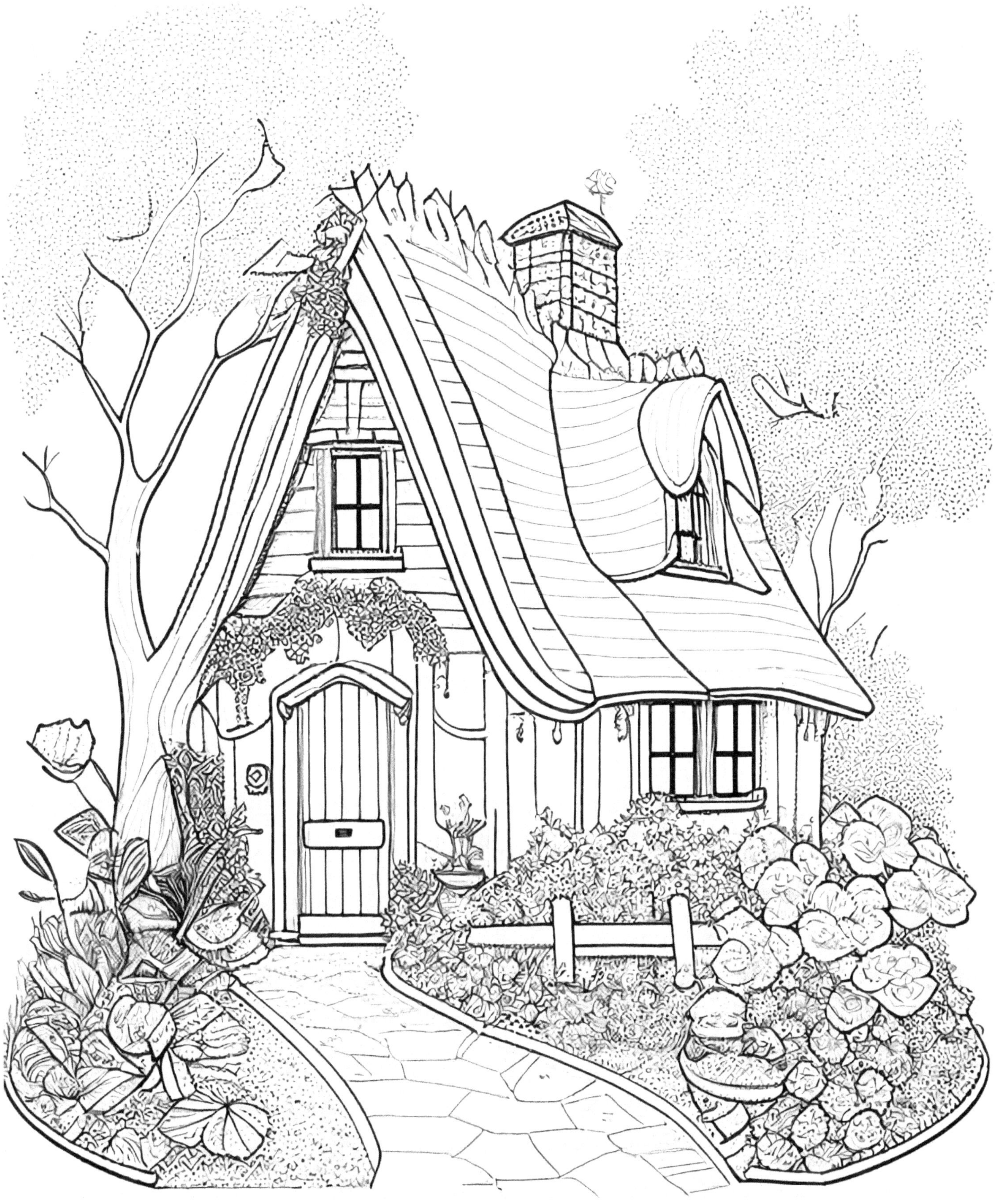

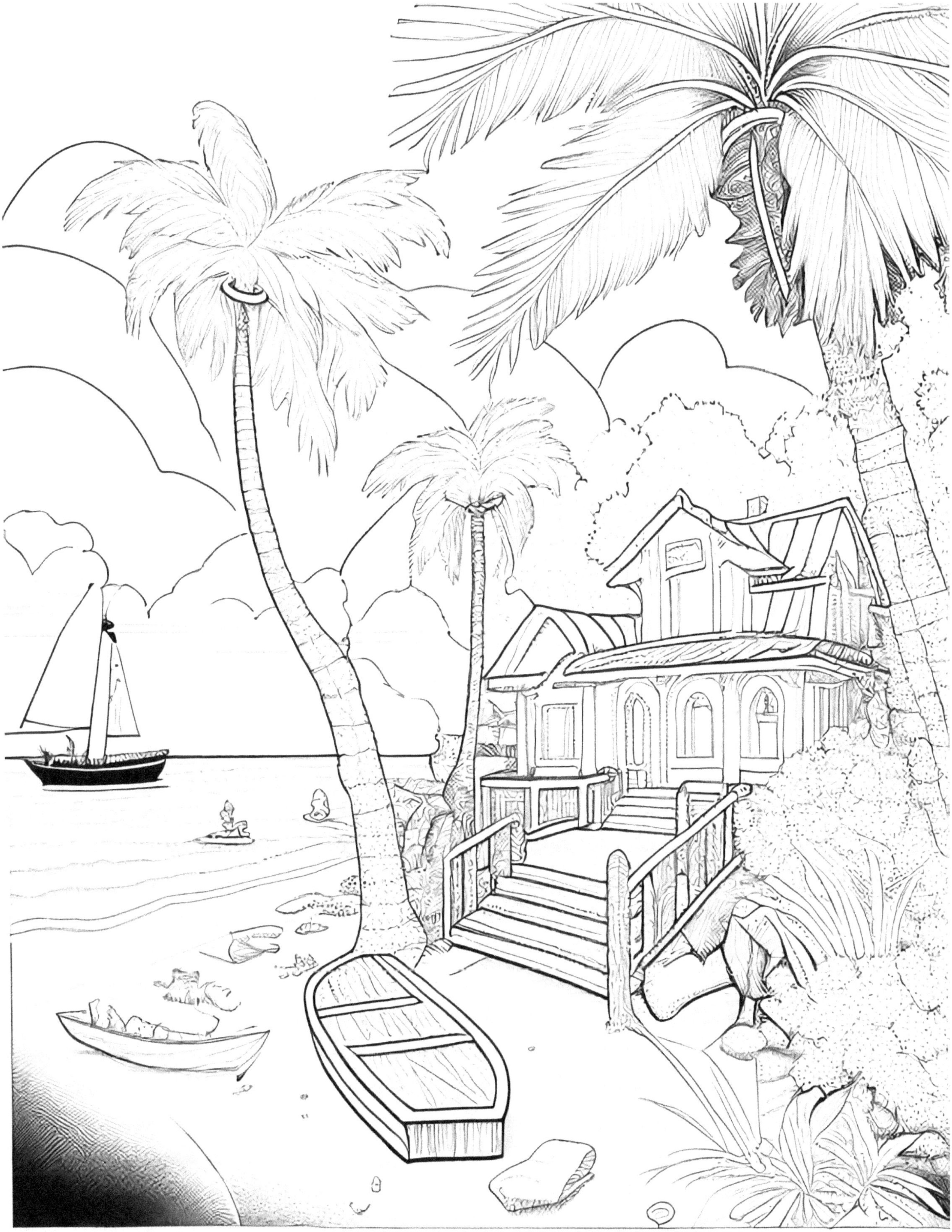

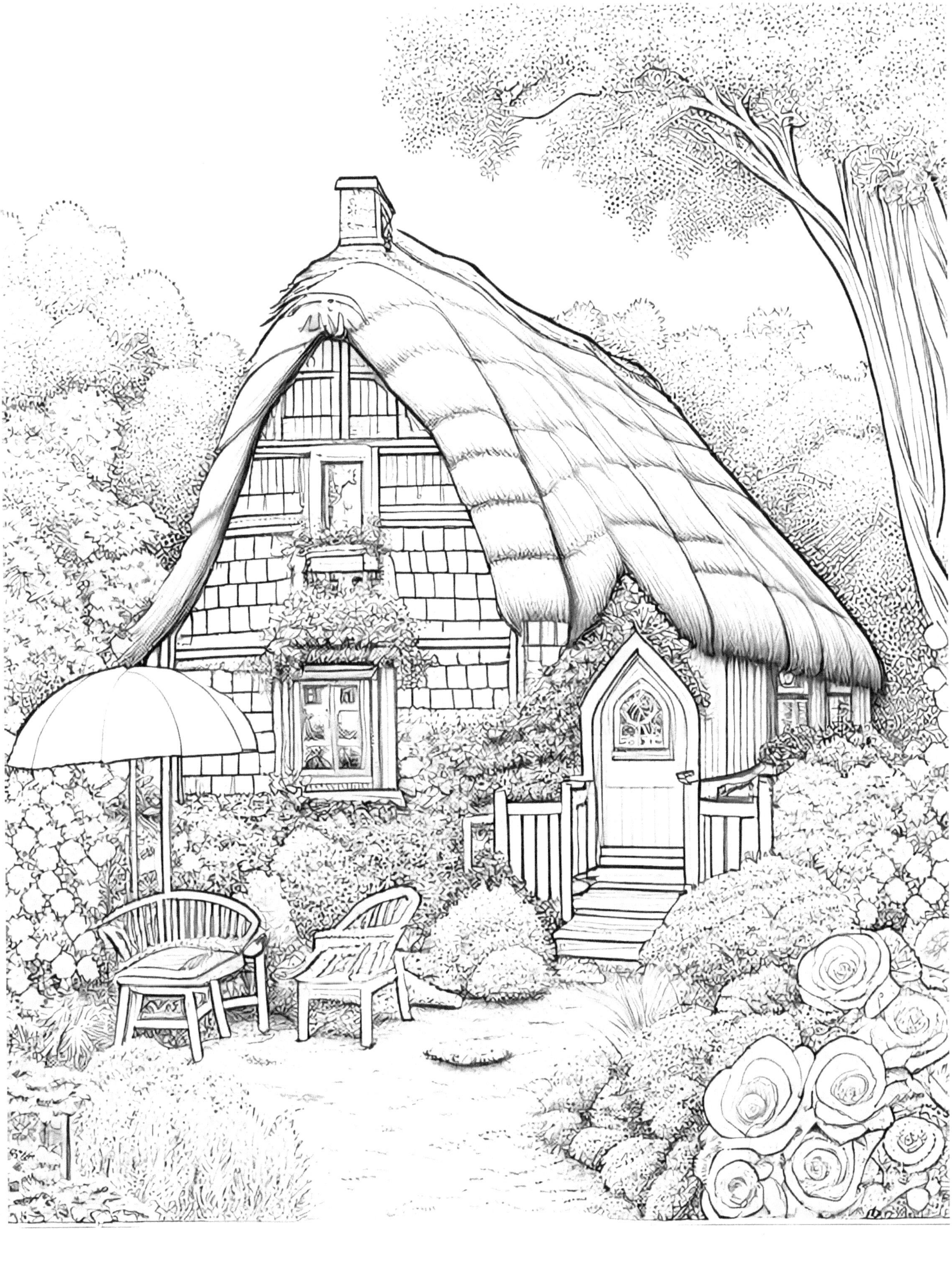

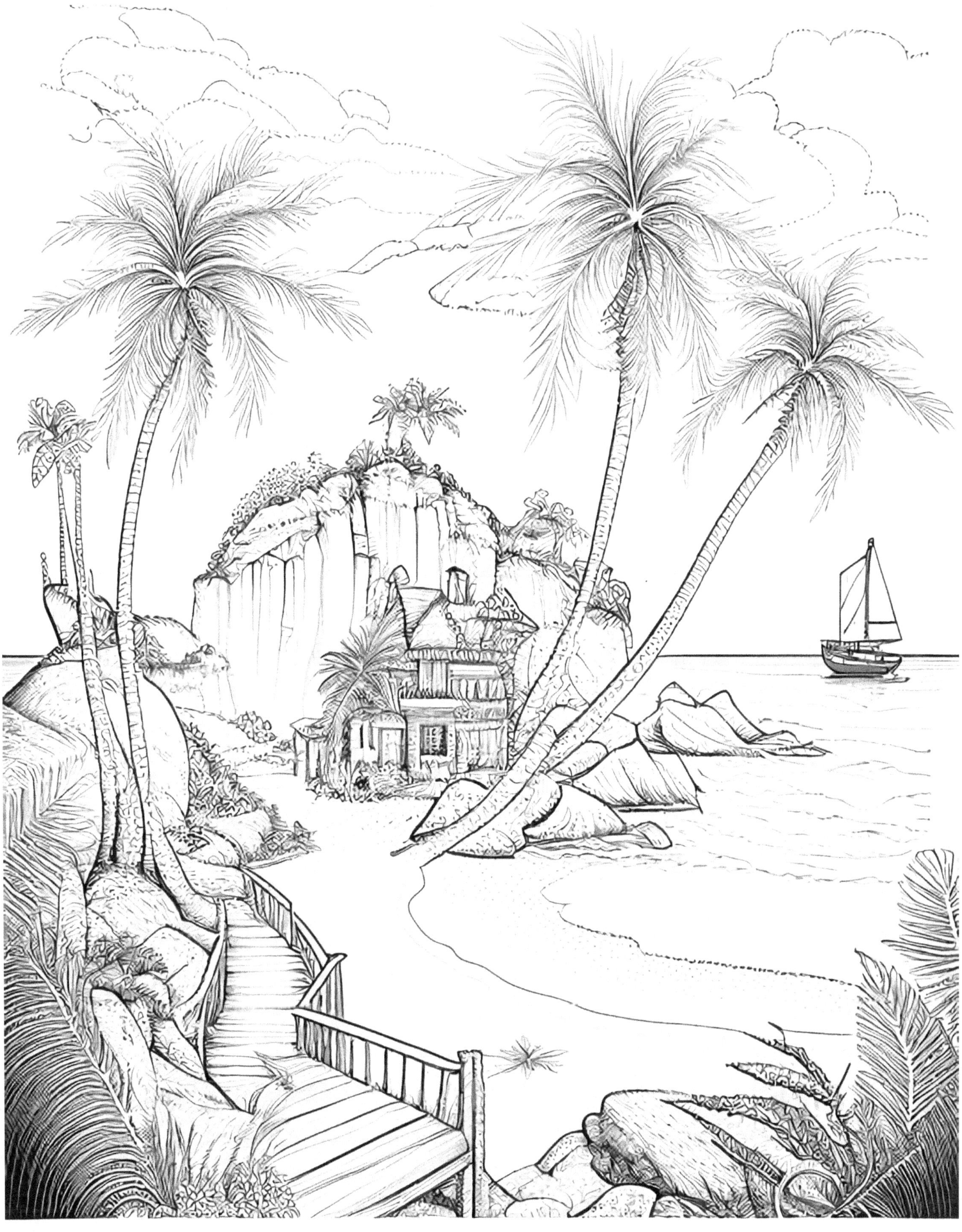

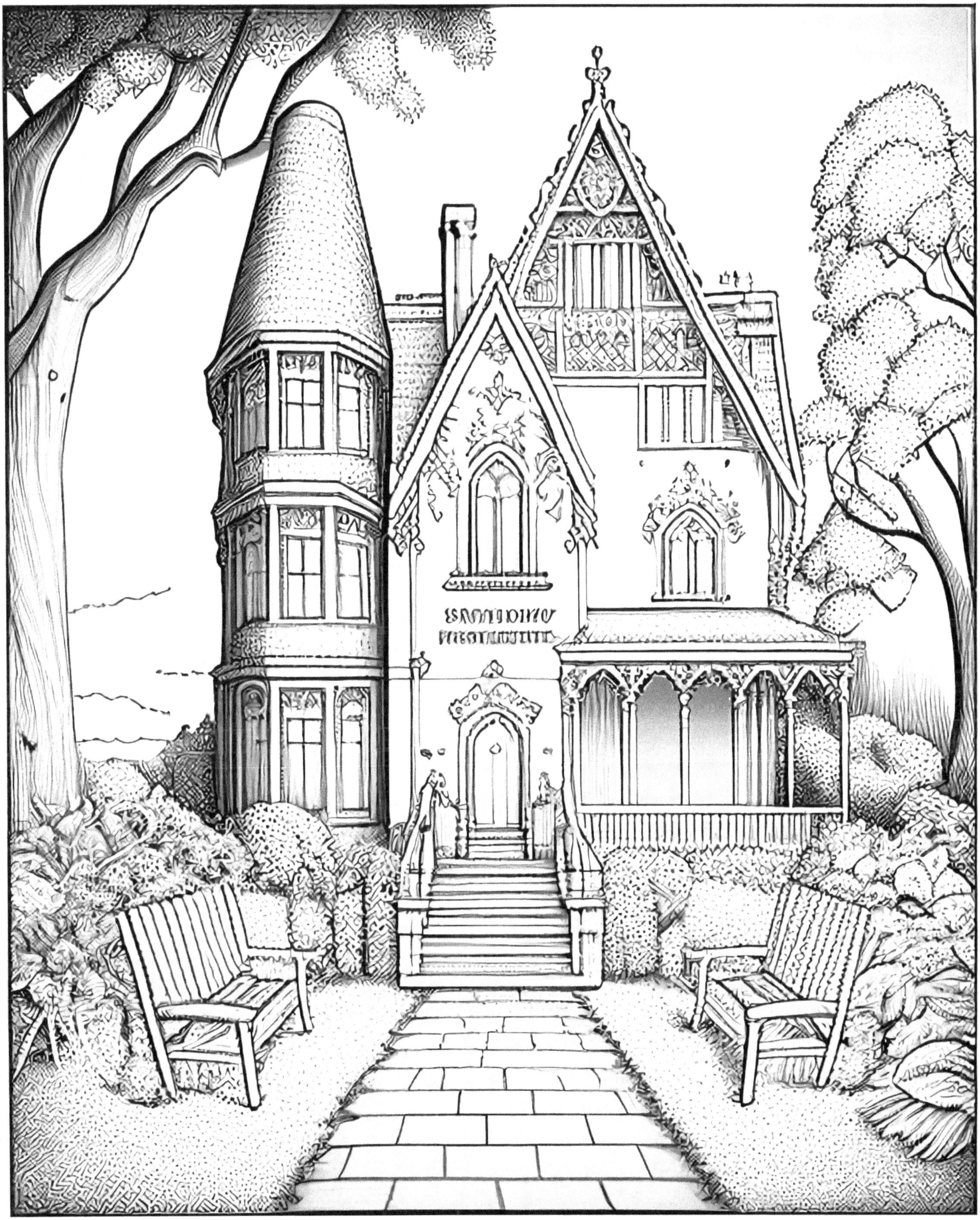

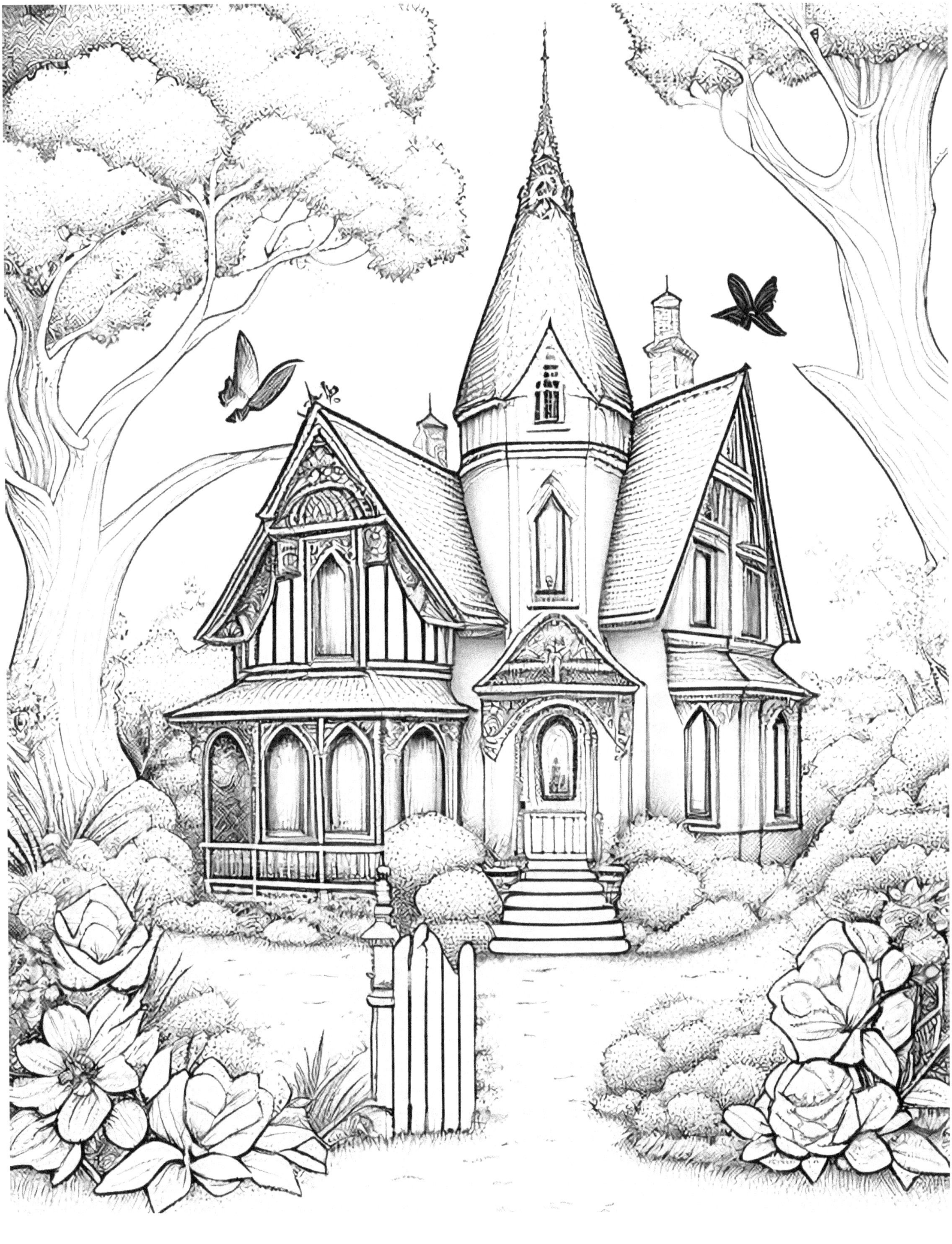

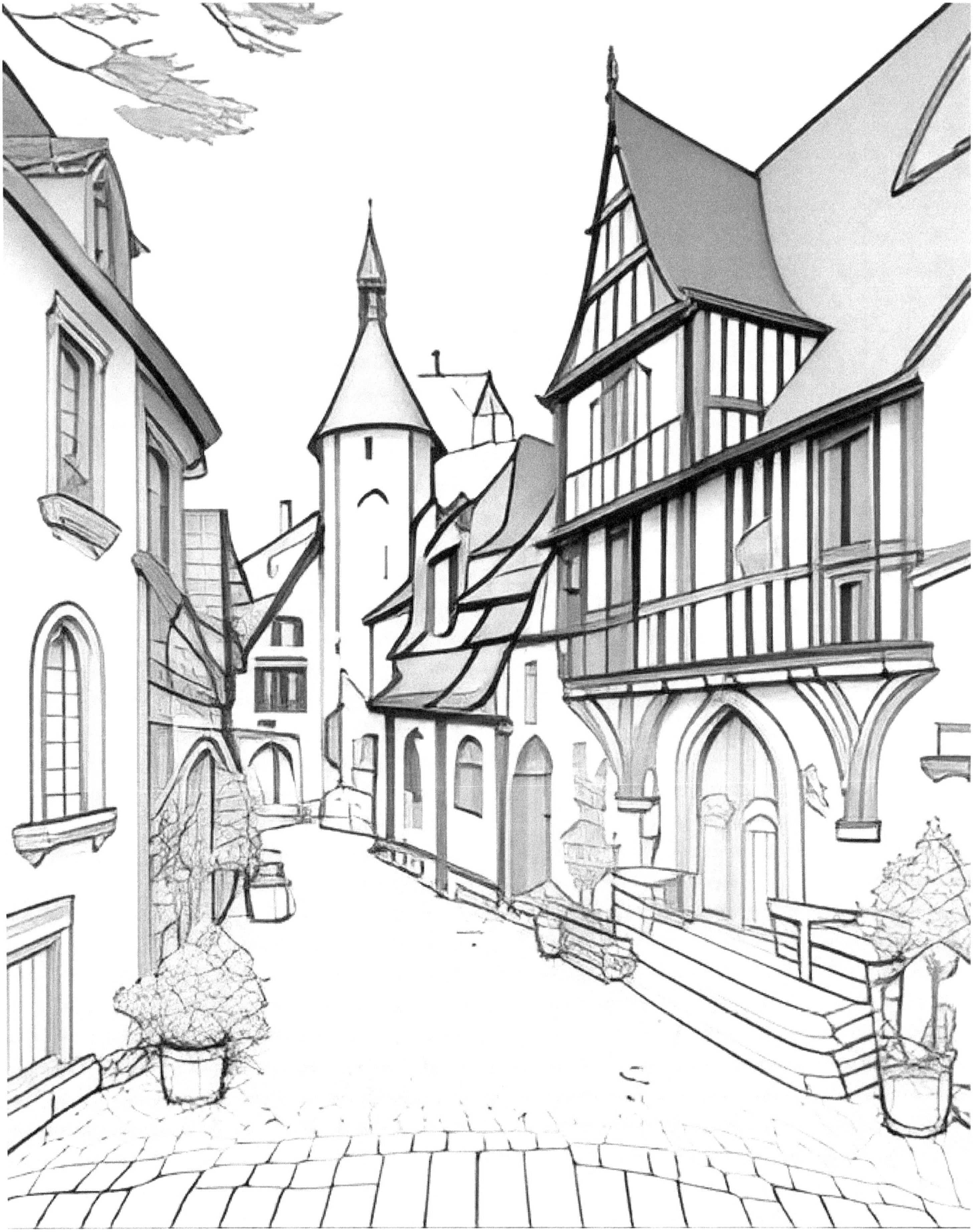

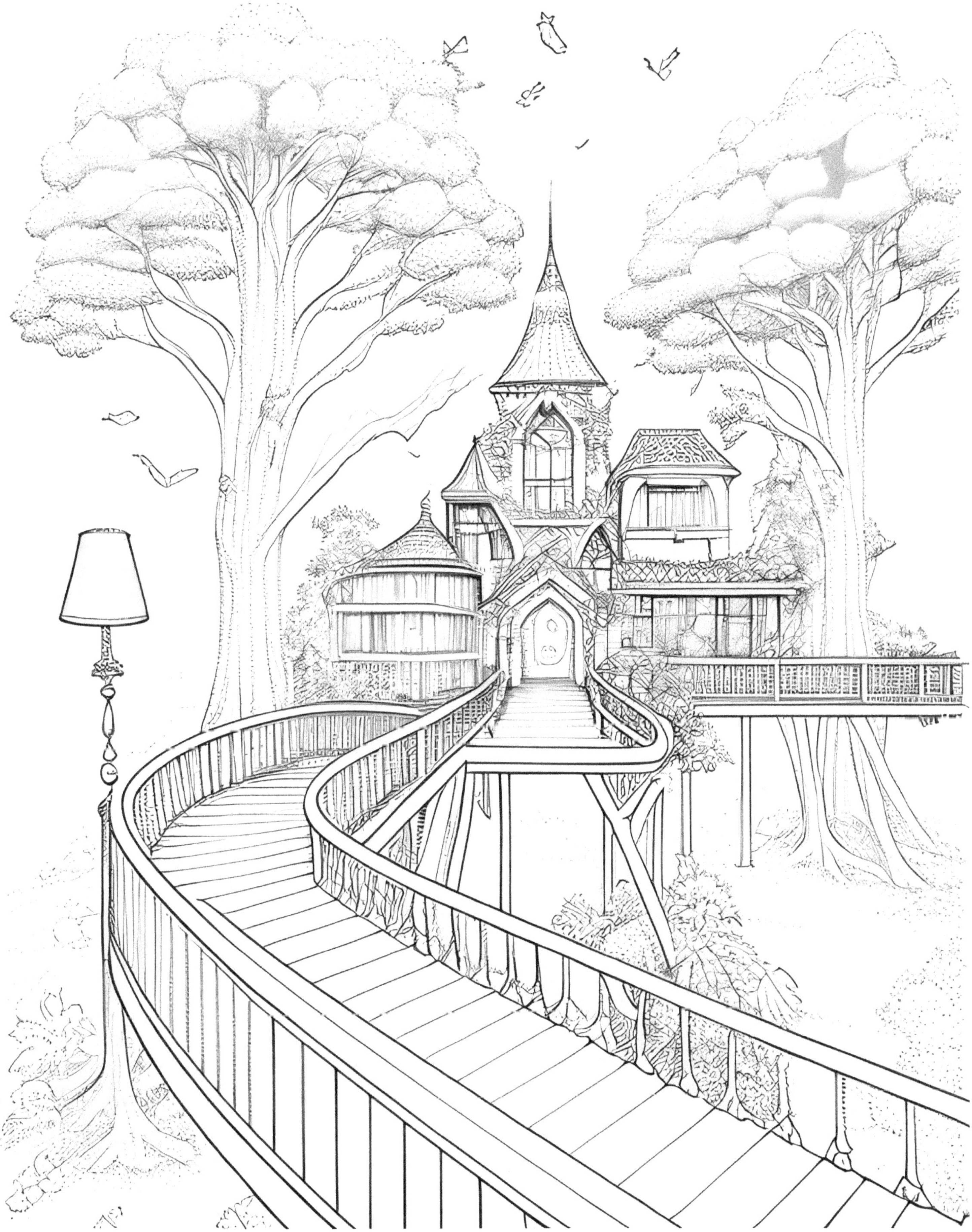

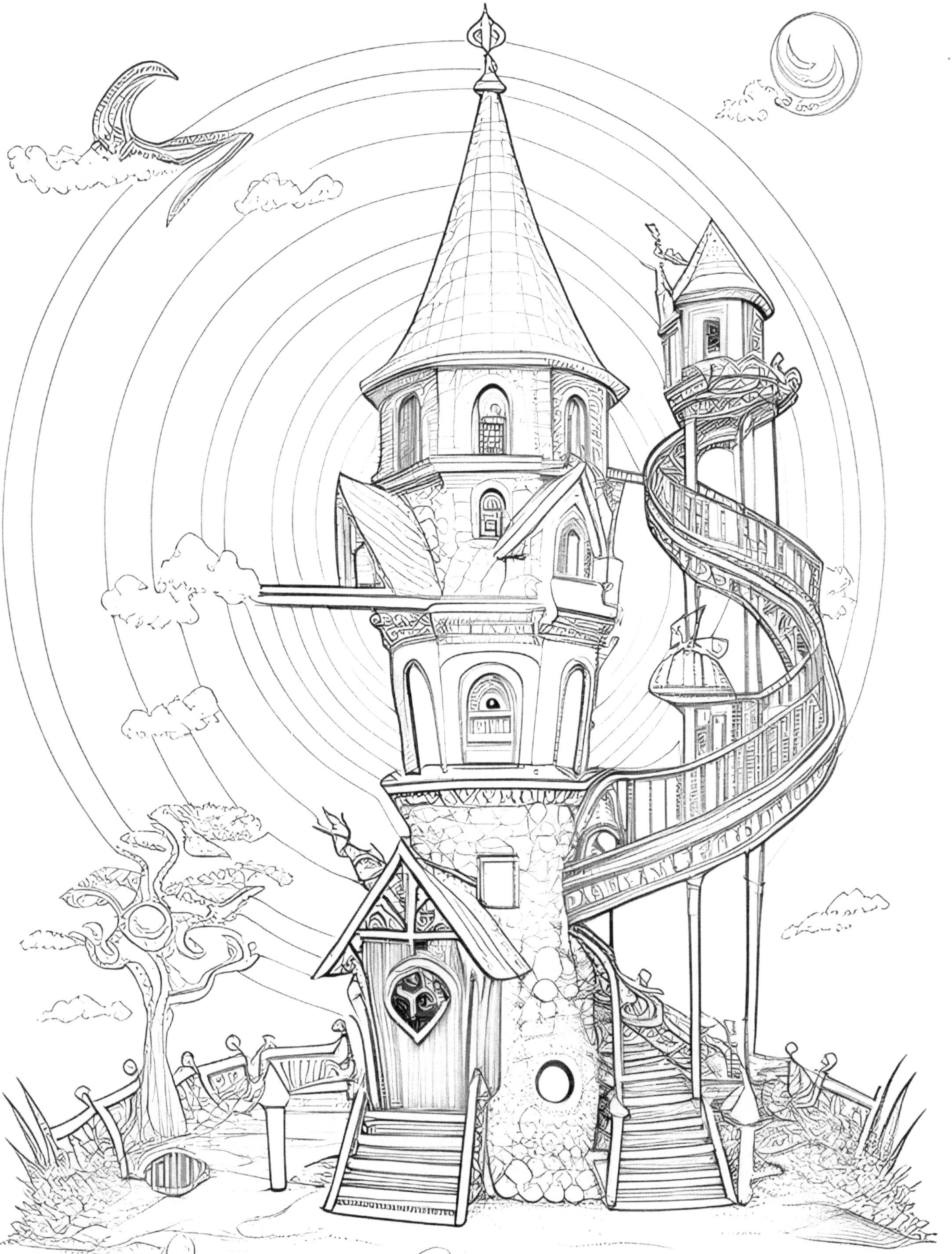

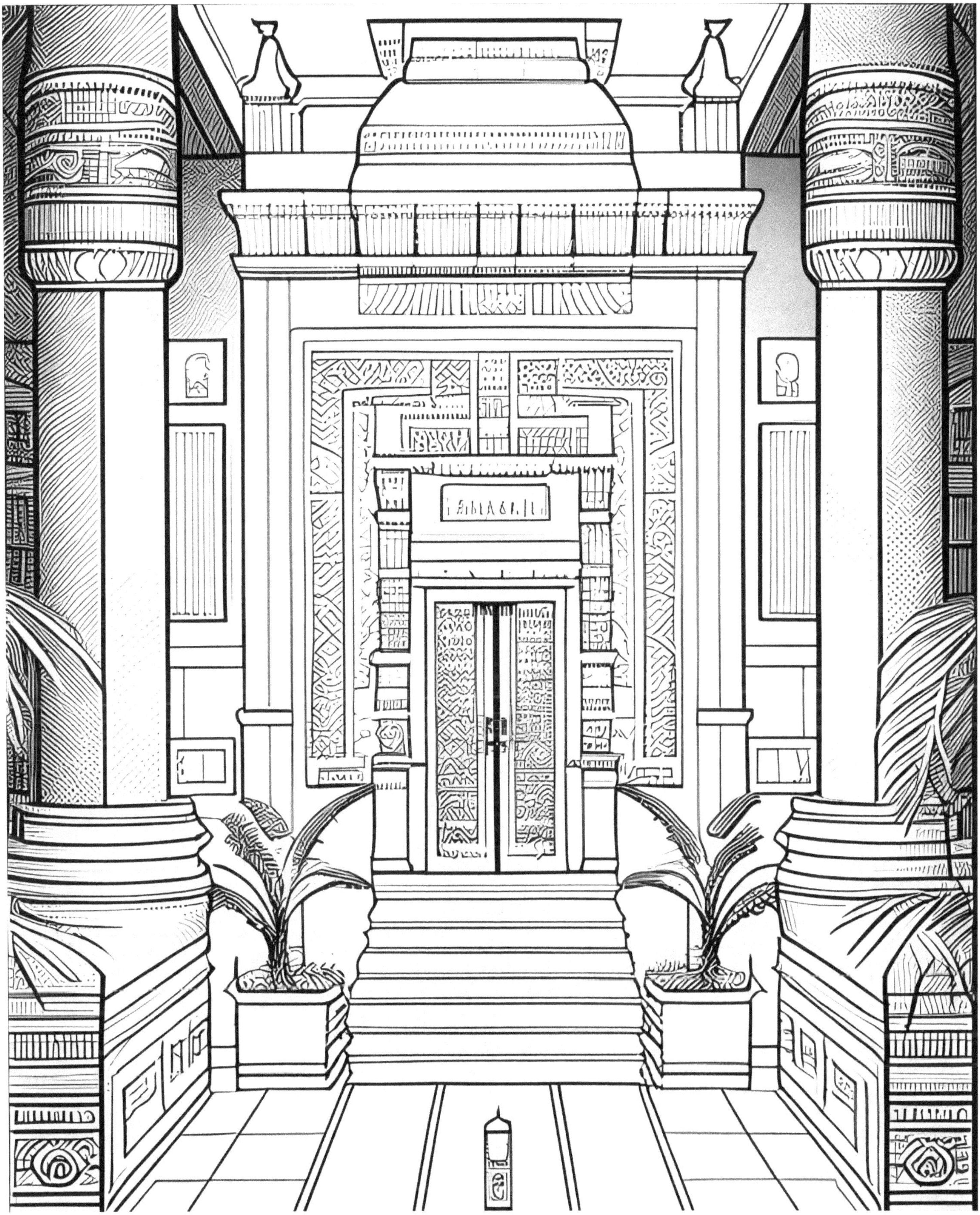

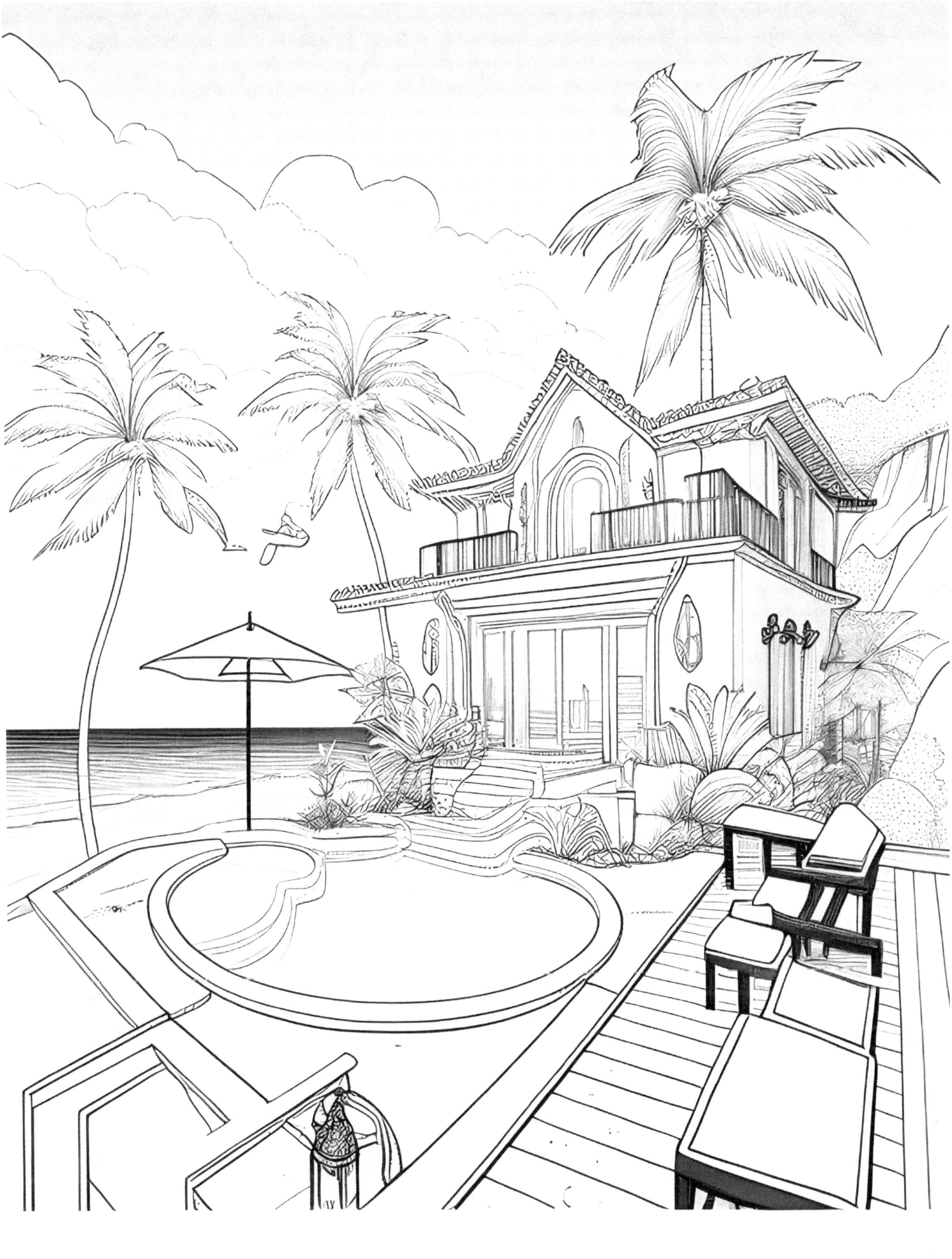

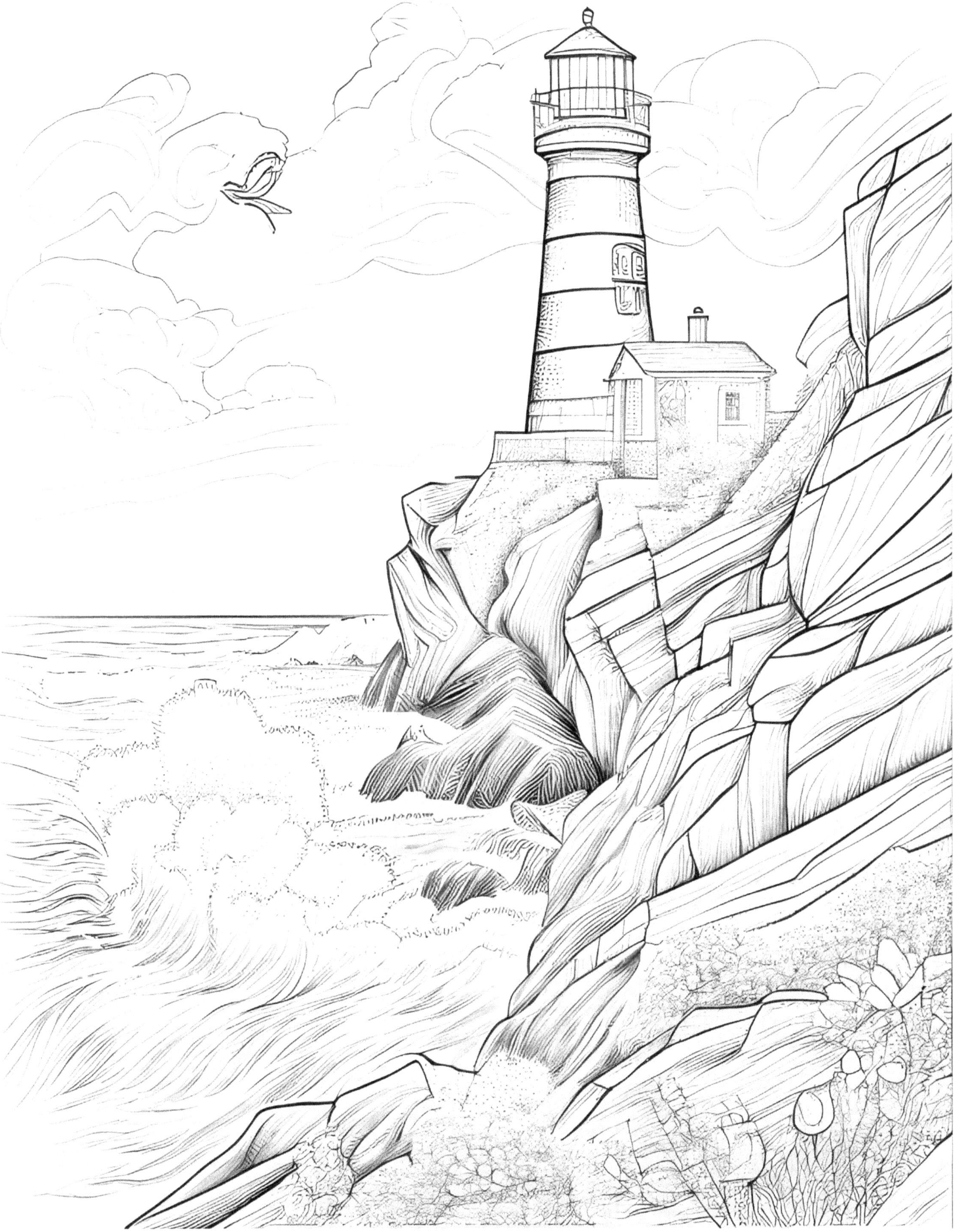

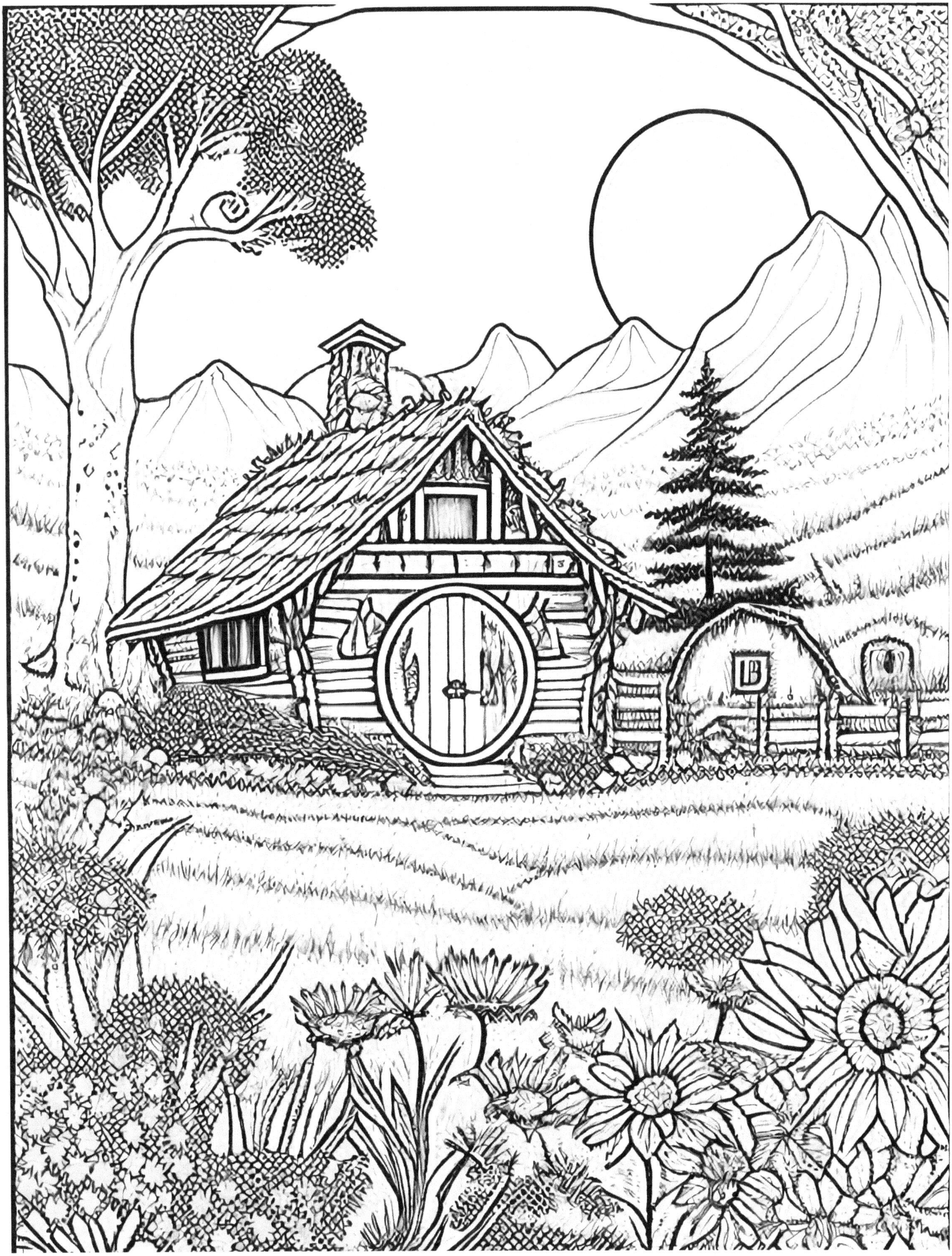

www.ingramcontent.com/pod-product-compliance
Lightning Source LLC
Chambersburg PA
CBHW080914220526
45467CB00024BA/2566
* 9 7 9 8 3 7 6 8 2 4 5 0 4 *